Law for Professionals

The *Law for Professionals* book series contains publications in all fields of the law aimed at professionals and practitioners. The book series is dedicated to publish high quality books that provide in-depth insights into the workings and the practical functioning of the law, international organizations or regional legal frameworks.

The authors contributing to the book series are experienced legal professionals and practitioners whose expertise combines theory and practice.

Robert H. D. Reimer

Packaging Policy and Circular Economy

The Packaging Legislation of the European Union under the European Green Deal

Springer

Robert H. D. Reimer
Cologne, Germany

ISSN 2662-141X ISSN 2662-1428 (electronic)
Law for Professionals
ISBN 978-3-032-27080-1 ISBN 978-3-032-27081-8 (eBook)
https://doi.org/10.1007/978-3-032-27081-8

This Springer imprint is published by the registered company Springer Nature Switzerland AG
The registered company address is: Gewerbestrasse 11, 6330 Cham, Switzerland

Competing Interests The author has no competing interests to declare that are relevant to the content of this manuscript.

Contents

Abbreviations

AbfallR	Zeitschrift für das Recht der Abfallwirtschaft (Journal)
Antr. Sci	Anthropocene Science (Journal)
ARSP	Archiv für Rechts- und Sozialphilosophie (Journal)
art.	Article(s)
Bd.	Band (engl.: Volume)
BEC	Banson Editorial and Communications Ltd
CEAP	Circular Economy Action Plan
CEN	Comité Européen de Normalisation (engl.: European Committee for Standardization)
CENIA	Česká informační agentura životního prostředí (engl.: Czech Environmental Information Agency)
CFR	Charter of Fundamental Rights of the European Union
ch.	Chapter
CID	Clean Industrial Deal
CJEU	Court of Justice of the European Union
Clean Techn Environ Policy	Clean Technologies and Environmental Policy (Journal)
CLPR	Regulation (EC) No 1272/2008 of the European Parliament and of the Council of 16 December 2008 on classification, labelling and packaging of substances and mixtures, amending and repealing Directives 67/548/EEC and 1999/45/EC, and amending Regulation (EC) No 1907/2006 (Text with EEA relevance), OJ L 353, 31.12.2008, p. 1, last amended by Commission Delegated Regulation (EU) 2023/1434 of 25 April 2023 amending, for the purposes of its adaptation to technical and scientific progress, Regulation (EC) No 1272/2008 of

	the European Parliament and of the Council on classification, labelling and packaging of substances and mixtures as regards the addition of notes to Part 1, section 1.1.3, of Annex VI (Text with EEA relevance), OJ L 176, 11.7.2023, p. 3 (Classification, Labelling, and Packaging Regulation)
COM	(European) Commission
COREPER	Committee of Permanent Representatives/ Comité des représentants permanents
CPA	Circular Plastics Alliance
CRP	Council Decision of 1 December 2009 adopting the Council's Rules of Procedure, OJ L 325, 11.12.2009, p. 35, last amended by Council Decision (EU, Euratom) 2023/2827 of 12 December 2023 amending the Council's Rules of Procedure, OJ L, 2023/2827, 14.12.2023 (Council of the European Union's Rules of Procedure)
CSCP	Collaborating Centre on Sustainable Consumption and Production
CSR	Corporate Social Responsibility
Cult. Organ.	Culture and Organization (Journal)
DG ENV	(European Commission) Directorate General for Environment
DG ENV.A	(European Commission) Directorate General for Environment—Directorate General Affairs, Knowledge and Resources
DG ENV.B	(European Commission) Directorate General for Environment—Directorate Circular Economy
DG ENV.B1	(European Commission) Directorate General for Environment—Directorate Circular Economy—Circular Economy, Sustainable Production and Consumption
DG ENV.B2	(European Commission) Directorate General for Environment—Directorate Circular Economy—Safe and Sustainable Chemicals
DG ENV.B3	(European Commission) Directorate General for Environment—Directorate Circular Economy—From Waste to Resources
DG ENV.B4	(European Commission) Directorate General for Environment—Directorate Circular Economy—Sustainable Products
DG ENV.C	(European Commission) Directorate General for Environment—Directorate Zero Pollution

DG ENV.D	(European Commission) Directorate General for Environment—Directorate Biodiversity
DG ENV.E	(European Commission) Directorate General for Environment—Directorate Compliance, Governance & Support to Member States
DG ENV.F	(European Commission) Directorate General for Environment—Directorate Green Diplomacy & Multilateralism
DIN	Deutsches Institut für Normung e.V. (engl.: German Institute for Standardization)
Directive (EU) 2018/851	Directive (EU) 2018/851 of the European Parliament and of the Council of 30 May 2018 amending Directive 2008/98/EC on waste, OJ L 150, 14.6.2018, p. 109.
EAP	Environment Action Programme(s) of the European Union
ECJ	European Court of Justice
ed(s).	Editor(s)/Edition(s)
EEA	European Environment Agency
EEAS	European External Action Service
EEELR	European Energy and Environmental Law Review (Journal)
EESC	European Economic and Social Committee
EGD	European Green Deal
Eionet	European Environment Information and Observation Network
EJDR	The European Journal of Development Research (Journal)
ENV	Council of the European Union's Environment Council
ENVI	European Parliament's Committee on Environment, Public Health and Food Safety
Environ Sci Policy	Environmental Science & Policy (Journal)
Environ. Innov. Soc. Transit.	Environmental Innovation and Societal Transitions (Journal)
EPPPL	European Procurement and Public-Private Partnership Law Review (Journal)
EPR	Extended Producer Responsibility
EPRS	European Parliamentary Research Service
ErPD	Directive 2009/125/EC of the European Parliament and of the Council of 21 October 2009 establishing a framework for the setting of ecodesign requirements for energy-related products, OJ L 285, 31.10.2009, p. 10, last amended by Directive 2012/27/EU of the European

	Parliament and of the Council of 25 October 2012 on energy efficiency, amending Directives 2009/125/EC and 2010/30/EU and repealing Directives 2004/8/EC and 2006/32/EC Text with EEA relevance, OJ L 315, 14.11.2012, p. 1 (Energy-Related Products Directive)
et al.	et alia (engl.: and others)
ETC CE	European Topic Centre on Circular Economy and Resource Use
ESEU	Environmental Science Europe (Journal)
ESPR	Regulation (EU) 2024/1781 of the European Parliament and of the Council of 13 June 2024 establishing a framework for the setting of ecodesign requirements for sustainable products, amending Directive (EU) 2020/1828 and Regulation (EU) 2023/1542 and repealing Directive 2009/125/EC, OJ L, 2024/1781, 28.6.2024 (Ecodesign for Sustainable Products Regulation)
EU	European Union
European Climate Law	Regulation (EU) 2021/1119 of the European Parliament and of the Council of 30 June 2021 establishing the framework for achieving climate neutrality and amending Regulations (EC) No 401/2009 and (EU) 2018/1999 ('European Climate Law'), OJ L 243, 9.7.2021, p. 1
EurUP	Europäisches Umwelt- und Planungsrecht (Journal)
Eur. Law J.	European Law Journal (Journal)
EuZW	Europäische Zeitschrift für Wirtschaftsrecht (Journal)
FCMFR	Regulation (EC) No 1935/2004 of the European Parliament and of the Council of 27 October 2004 on materials and articles intended to come into contact with food and repealing Directives 80/590/EEC and 89/109/EEC, OJ L 338, 13.11.2004, p. 4, last amended by Regulation (EU) 2019/1381 of the European Parliament and of the Council of 20 June 2019 on the transparency and sustainability of the EU risk assessment in the food chain and amending Regulations (EC) No 178/2002, (EC) No 1829/2003, (EC) No 1831/2003, (EC) No 2065/2003, (EC) No 1935/2004, (EC) No 1331/2008, (EC) No 1107/2009, (EU) 2015/2283 and Directive 2001/18/EC, OJ L 231, 6.9.2019, p. 1 (Food Contact Materials Framework Regulation)

G.A.	(United Nations) General Assembly
GACERE	Global Alliance on Circular Economy and Resource Efficiency
GC	Governing Council of the United Nations Environment Programme
GCC	Gulf Cooperation Council
GEG	Global Environmental Governance
Ger. Law J.	German Law Journal (Journal)
Glob Environ Change	Global Environmental Change (Journal)
GSC	General Secretariat of the Council of the European Union
HILJ	Harvard International Law Journal (Journal)
i.e.	id est (engl.: that is)
id.	idem (engl.: the same)
INC	(United Nations Environment Programme) Intergovernmental Negotiating Committee (on Plastic Pollution)
INC-1	First session of the (United Nations Environment Programme) Intergovernmental Negotiating Committee (on Plastic Pollution) in Punta del Este, Uruguay, from 28th November to 2nd December 2022
INC-2	Second session of the (United Nations Environment Programme) Intergovernmental Negotiating Committee (on Plastic Pollution) in Paris, France, from 29th May to 2nd June 2023
INC-3	Third session of the (United Nations Environment Programme) Intergovernmental Negotiating Committee (on Plastic Pollution) in Nairobi, Kenya, from 13th to 19th November 2023
INC-4	Fourth session of the (United Nations Environment Programme) Intergovernmental Negotiating Committee (on Plastic Pollution) in Ottawa, Canada, from 23rd to 29th April 2024
INC-5	Fifth session of the (United Nations Environment Programme) Intergovernmental Negotiating Committee (on Plastic Pollution) in Busan, Republic of Korea, from 25th November to 1st December 2024
IJEP	International Journal of Environment and Pollution (Journal)
IRCrES	Istituto di Ricerca sulla Crescita Economica Sostenibile del Consiglio Nazionale delle Ricerche (engl.: Research Institute on Sustainable Economic Growth of the National Research Council of Italy)

ISBB	International Sustainability Standards Board
ISO	International Organization for Standardization
J. Clean. Prod.	Journal of Cleaner Production (Journal)
J. Consum. Res.	Journal of Consumer Research (Journal)
J. Eur. Public Policy	Journal of European Public Policy (Journal)
J. Ind. Ecol.	Journal of Industrial Ecology (Journal)
JCMS	Journal of Common Market Studies (Journal)
KrWG	Gesetz zur Förderung der Kreislaufwirtschaft und Sicherung der umweltverträglichen Bewirtschaftung von Abfällen (Kreislaufwirtschaftsgesetz) vom 24. Februar 2012 (BGBl. I S. 212), das zuletzt durch Artikel 5 des Gesetzes vom 2. März 2023 (BGBl. 2023 I Nr. 56) geändert worden ist (engl.: (German) Circular Economy Act)
lit.	Litera (engl.: Letter)
Ltd	Limited
MSR	Regulation (EU) 2019/1020 of the European Parliament and of the Council of 20 June 2019 on market surveillance and compliance of products and amending Directive 2004/42/EC and Regulations (EC) No 765/2008 and (EU) No 305/2011, OJ L 169, 25.6.2019, p. 1, last amended by Regulation (EU) 2024/1252 of the European Parliament and of the Council of 11 April 2024 establishing a framework for ensuring a secure and sustainable supply of critical raw materials and amending Regulations (EU) No 168/2013, (EU) 2018/858, (EU) 2018/1724 and (EU) 2019/1020, OJ L, 2024/1252, 3.5.2024 (Market Surveillance Regulation)
NCPC	(Joint UNIDO/UNEP) National Cleaner Production Centre(s)
no.	Number(s)
NVwZ	Neue Zeitschrift für Verwaltungsrecht (Journal)
OECD	Organization for Economic Cooperation and Development
p./pp.	Page(s)
PACE	Platform for Accelerating the Circular Economy
PAGE	Partnership for Action on Green Economy
para(s).	Paragraph(s)
PAYT	Pay-as-you-throw (scheme)
PCSD	Policy Coherence for Sustainable Development
PEF	Product Environmental Footprint
PPA	Public Policy and Administration (Journal)

PPWD	European Parliament and Council Directive 94/62/EC of 20 December 1994 on packaging and packaging waste, OJ L 365, 31.12.1994, p. 10, last amended by Directive (EU) 2018/852 of the European Parliament and of the Council of 30 May 2018 amending Directive 94/62/EC on packaging and packaging waste, OJ L 150, 14.6.2018, p. 141 (Packaging and Packaging Waste Directive)
PPWR	Regulation (EU) 2025/40 of the European Parliament and of the Council of 19 December 2024 on packaging and packaging waste, amending Regulation (EU) 2019/1020 and Directive (EU) 2019/904, and repealing Directive 94/62/EC, OJ L, 2025/40, 22.1.2025 (Packaging and Packaging Waste Regulation)
PRO	Producer responsibility organization(s)
PRP	European Parliament, Rules of Procedure of the European Parliament, 2024–2029, 10th parliamentary term, July 2024 (European Parliament's Rules of Procedure)
pt(s).	Point(s)
RBC	Responsible Business Conduct
rec(s).	Recital(s)
RED II	Directive (EU) 2018/2001 of the European Parliament and of the Council of 11 December 2018 on the promotion of the use of energy from renewable sources, OJ L 328, 21.12.2018, p. 82, last amended by Directive (EU) 2024/1711 of the European Parliament and of the Council of 13 June 2024 amending Directives (EU) 2018/2001 and (EU) 2019/944 as regards improving the Union's electricity market design, OJ L, 2024/1711, 26.6.2024 (Renewable Energy Directive II)
Regulation (EC) No 401/2009	Regulation (EC) No 401/2009 of the European Parliament and of the Council of 23 April 2009 on the European Environment Agency and the European Environment Information and Observation Network (Codified version), OJ L 126 21.5.2009, p. 13, last amended by Regulation (EU) 2021/1119 of the European Parliament and of the Council of 30 June 2021 establishing the framework for achieving climate neutrality and

	amending Regulations (EC) No 401/2009 and (EU) 2018/1999 ('European Climate Law'), OJ L 243, 9.7.2021, p. 1
Res.	Resolution
Resour. Conserv. Recycl.	Resources, Conservation & Recycling (Journal)
RIW	Recht der internationalen Wirtschaft (Journal)
RJEA	Romanian Journal of European Affairs (Journal)
RPFCMR	Commission Regulation (EU) 2022/1616 of 15 September 2022 on recycled plastic materials and articles intended to come into contact with foods, and repealing Regulation (EC) No 282/2008, OJ L 243, 20.9.2022, p. 3, last amended by Corrigendum to Commission Regulation (EU) 2022/1616 of 15 September 2022 on recycled plastic materials and articles intended to come into contact with foods, and repealing Regulation (EC) No 282/2008 (Official Journal of the European Union L 243 of 20 September 2022), OJ L 244, 21.9.2022, p. 70 (Recycled Plastic Food Contact Materials Regulation)
Scie Bull	Scientific Bulletin of the Nicolae Balcescu Land Forces Academy, Sibiu, Romania
SCP	Sustainable Consumption and Production (Journal)
SDG	(United Nations 2030 Agenda) Sustainable Development Goal(s)
SEEDS	Sustainable Environmental Economics and Dynamics Studies (Journal)
sq.	sequens/sequensque (engl.: the following (singular))
sqq.	sequentes/sequentesque (engl.: the following (plural))
STOA	(European Parliamentary Research Service) Panel for the Future of Science and Technology (Scientific Foresight Unit)
StoffR	Zeitschrift für Stoffrecht (Journal)
subpara(s).	Subparagraph(s)
SUP	Single-Use Plastic(s)
SUPD	Directive (EU) 2019/904 of the European Parliament and of the Council of 5 June 2019 on the reduction of the impact of certain plastic products on the environment, OJ L 155, 12.6.2019 (Single-Use Plastics Directive)

Sustain. Prod. Consum.	Sustainable Production and Consumption (Journal)
SWD	Staff Working Document
TEU	Treaty on the European Union
TFEU	Treaty on the Functioning of the European Union
TREE	Directorate Environment, Education, Transport, Telecom and Energy of the General Secretariat of the Council of the European Union
TREE.1	Unit Environment, Education, Youth, Culture, Audiovisual and Sport of the Directorate Environment, Education, Transport, Telecom and Energy of the General Secretariat of the Council of the European Union
TREE.1.A	Sector Environment and Climate Change of the Unit Environment, Education, Youth, Culture, Audiovisual and Sport of the Directorate Environment, Education, Transport, Telecom and Energy of the General Secretariat of the Council of the European Union
UBA	Umweltbundesamt (engl.: (German) Federal Environment Agency)
UN	United Nations
UNC	Charter of the United Nations
UNEA	United Nations Environment Assembly
UNEO	United Nations Environment Organization
UNEP	United Nations Environment Programme
UNEPO	United Nations Environment Protection Organization
UNIDO	United Nations Industrial Development Organization
UWWTD	Directive (EU) 2024/3019 of the European Parliament and of the Council of 27 November 2024 concerning urban wastewater treatment (recast), OJ L 2024/3019, 12.12.2024, last amended by Corrigendum to Directive (EU) 2024/3019 of the European Parliament and of the Council of 27 November 2024 concerning urban wastewater treatment (OJ L 2024/3019, 12.12.2024), OJ L 2025/90038, 16.1.2025 (Urban Wastewater Treatment Directive)
VITO	Vlaamse Instelling voor Technologisch Onderzoek
Vol.	Volume
VTT	Teknologian tutkimuskeskus VTT Oy (engl.: Technical Research Centre of Finland)

Waste Manage.	Waste Management (Journal)
WCEF	World Circular Economy Forum
WEO	World Environment Organization
WFD	Directive 2008/98/EC of the European Parliament and of the Council of 19 November 2008 on waste and repealing certain Directives, OJ L 312, 22.11.2008, p. 3, last amended by Directive (EU) 2025/1892 of the European Parliament and of the Council of 10 September 2025 amending Directive 2008/98/EC on waste, OJ L 2025/1982, 26.9.2025 (Waste Framework Directive)
WHO	World Health Organization
WI	Wuppertal Institut
WPO	World Packaging Organisation
WRFA	World Resources Forum Association
WTO	World Trade Organization
Zbornik PFZ	Zbornik Pravnog Fakulteta u Zagreb (Journal)
ZUR	Zeitschrift für Umweltrecht (Journal)
10YFP/OPN	10-Year Framework of Programmes on Sustainable Consumption and Production Patterns/One Planet Network

1 Introduction

Abstract

Packaging has emerged as one of the most strategically significant interfaces between economic activity and environmental protection. What was once regarded as a technical segment of waste law now constitutes a central regulatory field within the EU's Circular Economy transition and is a structural component of the EU's transformation towards climate neutrality and sustainable resource use. Since the regulatory framework has become increasingly dense, complex and interconnected, the EU's strategic policy agendas, especially the European Green Deal, the Clean Industrial Deal, and the New Circular Economy Action Plan, come into focus and imply a comprehensive examination of the European conceptualization and operationalization to tackle packaging and packaging waste in a truly Circular Economy.

Packaging has become one of the most visible and contested interfaces between modern economies and environmental limits. Few regulatory fields illustrate as clearly how abstract sustainability objectives translate into concrete obligations affecting daily business operations, consumer choices and public infrastructure. From product design decisions and supply-chain organisation to reporting duties, market access and reputational exposure, packaging regulation increasingly shapes strategic considerations across industries. For practitioners working in packaging, waste management, sustainability governance or regulatory compliance, the Circular Economy transition is therefore not a distant policy aspiration but an immediate and evolving operational reality. In tandem with this development, Packaging Policy has moved to the centre of broader political and economic debates. What was once largely perceived as a technical sub-area of waste law is now closely linked to questions of industrial competitiveness, resource security, innovation capacity and

R. H. D. Reimer, *Packaging Policy and Circular Economy*, Law for Professionals, https://doi.org/10.1007/978-3-032-27081-8_1

global environmental leadership. The EU's regulatory initiatives in this field signal a shift from incremental environmental legislation towards a systemic transformation of material use and value chains. This shift affects not only how packaging is produced and managed at end-of-life, but also how responsibilities are allocated between public authorities, producers, consumers and downstream actors in increasingly complex governance arrangements. The growing density of rules, strategies and policy initiatives, however, also creates uncertainty. Economic actors face the challenge of navigating a rapidly evolving legal landscape in which Packaging Policy intersects with climate law, product regulation, industrial policy and international sustainability frameworks. Non-governmental organizations and civil society actors must assess whether regulatory ambition is matched by effective implementation, while public authorities at European, national and local levels are required to coordinate policies across jurisdictions and administrative silos. Therefore, there is a growing demand among practitioners and decision-makers for structured, legally sound and policy-oriented analysis that clarifies how European Packaging Policy is conceptualised, operationalised and embedded within the broader Circular Economy transition. This analysis responds to that demand by situating European Packaging Policy within its socio-economic, political and legal context and by unpacking the mechanisms through which policy objectives are translated into binding legal frameworks. It addresses Packaging Policy not as an isolated regulatory domain, but as a dynamic and multi-level system shaped by international commitments, European governance structures and national implementation practices. By doing so, it seeks to bridge the gap between strategic policy discourse and the practical realities faced by actors operating along the packaging value chain.

Against this backdrop, Packaging Policy is examined as a cornerstone of the Circular Economy and as a vehicle in the transformation process towards an equilibrium of sustainability and prosperity. Taking into account that the EU has defined this equilibrium in particular via its European Green Deal, the question arises how Europe ensures the Circular Economy transition by formulating and implementing the European Green Deal agenda in the field of European Packaging Policy and European Packaging Legislation. Since European Packaging Policy and Legislation have been shaped through various policy conceptualizations and legal acts, the analysis relies on a precise and detailed evaluation of the EU's corresponding agenda-setting and instrument selection in the policy-making process. Thus, the spotlight must be turned on the concretization and systematization of the EU's objectives and measures, which accordingly characterize European Packaging Policy. In this respect, the EU's involvement in the international community under the UN relevant frameworks for Packaging Policy and Circular Economy (§ 1), the identification of European Environmental Governance Actors and assessment of their role (§ 2), the preconditions for European Packaging Legislation (§ 3), the evaluation of the essential European Packaging Policy conceptions (§ 4), and the distinctive features of the current European Packaging Law Revision (§ 5) are determining factors for the characterization of European Packaging Policy.

To translate this analytical focus into a coherent and transparent examination, the structure of the study follows a stepwise approach. Building on the identification and systematisation of objectives, actors and instruments that characterize European Packaging Policy, the analysis proceeds from the international level to the European governance framework and ultimately to the current legislative consolidation. This progression reflects the multi-level nature of Packaging Policy and Circular Economy governance and allows the interaction between normative frameworks, institutional actors, legal foundations, and policy concepts to be assessed in a structured and comprehensive manner. Accordingly, the study proceeds in essence as follows:

The first chapter contains an analysis of the UN 2030 agenda, the UN sustainable development goals, the UN environment programme, the UN environment assembly, and the UN plastic pollution treaty. In the second chapter, the role of the European Commission's Circular Economy Directorate and Green Diplomacy and Multilateralism Directorate, the European External Action Service, the European Environment Agency, and the European Parliament's Committee on the Environment, Public Health and Food Safety, and the European Parliamentary Research Service will be elaborated. The third chapter will lay the focus on the legal basis, the basic principles, the regulatory system and the typical policy instruments of European Packaging Legislation. In the fourth chapter, the European Green Deal, the Clean Idustrial Deal, the New Circular Economy Action Plan, and the European Strategy for Plastics will be evaluated as essentials of European Packaging Policy conceptions. The fifth chapter will shed some light on the context, structure, and characteristics of the current European Packaging Law Revision. In the sixth chapter, conclusions will be drawn by summarizing the key findings of the analysis and by giving a prospect on the future development of Packaging Policy and Circular Economy.

United Nations

2

Abstract

Packaging Policy and the Circular Economy are regulated across international, national, and regional levels. Within this context, the international legal and political framework has an guiding effect for national and supranational actors. Against this backdrop, European Packaging Policy operates within a framework of international environmental governance shaped by the United Nations and its associated institutions. Central reference points include the UN 2030 Agenda for Sustainable Development, the Sustainable Development Goals (SDGs), the United Nations Environment Programme (UNEP), the United Nations Environment Assembly (UNEA), and the negotiations towards a global treaty on plastic pollution (UN Plastic Pollution Treaty). These instruments and fora establish normative principles, policy objectives, and procedural mechanisms that influence national and regional regulatory approaches. In particular, sustainable consumption and production, waste prevention, recycling, and life-cycle thinking constitute core elements of the international agenda relevant to packaging and plastics. The UN framework provides both substantive guidance and political impetus for the development of European Packaging Policy, ensuring coherence between regional regulation and global environmental commitments.

The EU's Packaging Policy tackles a problem of global relevance. Therefore, it must assure legal compliance to the respective obligations under international law, especially international treaties and common law. In order to preserve the consistency of universal and regional international policies, the EU must also ensure coherence with international frameworks, when it formulates a genuine European

R. H. D. Reimer, *Packaging Policy and Circular Economy*, Law for Professionals, https://doi.org/10.1007/978-3-032-27081-8_2

Packaging Policy. Behind this backdrop, the UN have, among others,[1] launched several approaches, including various international policy frameworks concerning the environment, which function as a guideline for European Packaging Policy. Considering the entangeld system of different intenational environment treaties and the fragmentary structure of internationally organized work on global environmental policies, Packaging Policy is a topic, located in between several UN environment policies and fora, especially the United Nations 2030 Agenda, the United Nations Sustainable Development Goals, the United Nations Environment Programme, the United Nations Environment Assembly, and the United Nations Plastic Pollution Treaty.

2.1 United Nations 2030 Agenda

On 25th September 2015, the UN General Assembly adopted its resolution A/RES/70/1 under the heading "Transforming our world: the 2030 Agenda for Sustainable Development".[2] It builds upon the Millennium Development Goals[3] of the Millennium Declaration[4] and refers to prominent international environmental actions,[5] especially the Rio Declaration on Environment and Development,[6] the World Summit on Sustainable Development, and the UN Conference on Sustainable Development. By stressing out that "[t]he future of humanity and of our planet lies in our hands[7]", whilst "we may be the last to have a chance of saving the planet[8]",

[1] See OECD (2022), Global Plastics Outlook, 22 February 2022. See furthermore also the frameworks of internationally organized private entities, for instance the ISBB, ISO or WPO.

[2] UN General Assembly (2015), Transforming our world: the 2030 Agenda for Sustainable Development, G.A. Res. A/RES/70/1 (21 October 2015).

[3] UN General Assembly (2015), Transforming our world: the 2030 Agenda for Sustainable Development, G.A. Res. A/RES/70/1 (21 October 2015), paras. 2, 10, 16, 17.

[4] UN General Assembly (2000), UN Millennium Declaration, G.A. RES/55/2 (18 September 2000).

[5] UN General Assembly (2015), Transforming our world: the 2030 Agenda for Sustainable Development, G.A. Res. A/RES/70/1 (21 October 2015), paras. 11 sq.

[6] UN General Assembly (1992), Report of the UN Conference on Environment and Development, Rio de Janeiro, 3–14 June 1992, G.A. Report A/CONF.151/26, Vol. I, Resolutions adopted by the Conference (UN publication, Sales No. E.93.I.8 and corrigendum), Resolution 1, Annex I.

[7] UN General Assembly (2015), Transforming our world: the 2030 Agenda for Sustainable Development, G.A. Res. A/RES/70/1 (21 October 2015), para. 53.

[8] UN General Assembly (2015), Transforming our world: the 2030 Agenda for Sustainable Development, G.A. Res. A/RES/70/1 (21 October 2015), para. 50.

and that the 2030 Agenda "is a charter for people and planet in the twenty-first centuary[9]", it highlights the outstanding relvance of the document, which is designated to not only the UN Member State's Governments, but also—under the auspices of a revitalized Global Partnership for Sustainable Development in a spirit of global solidarity[10]—civil society, the private sector, the UN systems, and other actors[11] as a plan of action for people, planet, and prosperity[12] for the 15 years period between 2015 and 2030.[13]

Laying the focus on Packaging Policy, the 2030 Agenda aims to protect the planet from degradation, including through sustainable consumption and production, sustainably managing its natural resources and taking action on climate change.[14] Therefore, it announces a new agenda of 17 Sustainable Development Goals with 169 associated targets.[15] Seeking to build strong economic foundations and to increase sustainable industrial development,[16] the 2030 Agenda is committed to making fundamental changes in the way that our societies produce and consume goods and services,[17] since social and economic development depends on the sustainable management of our planet's natural resources.[18] The 2030 Agenda considers achieving such a sustainable urban development and management, among other measures, through reduction and recycling of waste.[19]

[9] UN General Assembly (2015), Transforming our world: the 2030 Agenda for Sustainable Development, G.A. Res. A/RES/70/1 (21 October 2015), para. 51.

[10] UN General Assembly (2015), Transforming our world: the 2030 Agenda for Sustainable Development, G.A. Res. A/RES/70/1 (21 October 2015), paras. 39, 60 sqq.

[11] UN General Assembly (2015), Transforming our world: the 2030 Agenda for Sustainable Development, G.A. Res. A/RES/70/1 (21 October 2015), para. 60.

[12] UN General Assembly (2015), Transforming our world: the 2030 Agenda for Sustainable Development, G.A. Res. A/RES/70/1 (21 October 2015), preamble para. 1.

[13] UN General Assembly (2015), Transforming our world: the 2030 Agenda for Sustainable Development, G.A. Res. A/RES/70/1 (21 October 2015), preamble para. 4, paras. 3, 21, 47, 51, 72.

[14] UN General Assembly (2015), Transforming our world: the 2030 Agenda for Sustainable Development, G.A. Res. A/RES/70/1 (21 October 2015), preamble para. 6.

[15] UN General Assembly (2015), Transforming our world: the 2030 Agenda for Sustainable Development, G.A. Res. A/RES/70/1 (21 October 2015), preamble para. 3, para. 18, pp. 14 sqq.

[16] UN General Assembly (2015), Transforming our world: the 2030 Agenda for Sustainable Development, G.A. Res. A/RES/70/1 (21 October 2015), para. 27.

[17] UN General Assembly (2015), Transforming our world: the 2030 Agenda for Sustainable Development, G.A. Res. A/RES/70/1 (21 October 2015), para. 28.

[18] UN General Assembly (2015), Transforming our world: the 2030 Agenda for Sustainable Development, G.A. Res. A/RES/70/1 (21 October 2015), para. 33.

[19] UN General Assembly (2015), Transforming our world: the 2030 Agenda for Sustainable Development, G.A. Res. A/RES/70/1 (21 October 2015), para. 34.

2.2 United Nations Sustainable Development Goals

Among the UN 2030 Agenda Sustainable Development Goals (SDG),[20] Packaging Policy is predominantely covered by Goal 12, that demands to "[e]nsure sustainable consumption and production patterns[21]". As a general measure to achieve Goal 12, the 10-Year Framework of Programmes on Sustainable Consumption and Production Patterns[22] shall be implemented.[23] The sustainable management and efficient use of natural resources can be considered as a guiding principle,[24] which is concretized in the environmentally sound management of all wastes throughout their life circle by 2020[25] and the substantial reduction of waste generation through prevention, reduction, recycling, and reuse by 2030.[26] Hence, SDG 12 is affiliated with similar approaches, that are cogging on the international, regional, and national level of legislation, such as the concepts of a Green Economy and Green Growth under the UNEP Global Green New Deal.[27]

2.3 United Nations Environment Programme

The establishment of the UN Environment Programme (UNEP) roots in the outcomes of the UN Conference on the Human Environment in Stockholm in 1972,[28] namely the 27 principles of the Stockholm Declaration.[29] It is composed of eight divisions (industry and economy, ecosystems, law, early warning and assessment, climate change, communication, policy and programme, and corporate services) and an executive office.[30] UNEP functions as secretariat for several multilateral environmental agreements and other entities, for instance as secretariat of the

[20] UN General Assembly (2015), Transforming our world: the 2030 Agenda for Sustainable Development, G.A. Res. A/RES/70/1 (21 October 2015), pp. 14 sqq.

[21] UN General Assembly (2015), Transforming our world: the 2030 Agenda for Sustainable Development, G.A. Res. A/RES/70/1 (21 October 2015), p. 22.

[22] UN (2012), Agenda item 10 of the UN Conference on Sustainable Development, Rio de Janeiro, 20–22 June 2012, A/CONF.216/L.1.

[23] UN General Assembly (2015), Transforming our world: the 2030 Agenda for Sustainable Development, G.A. Res. A/RES/70/1 (21 October 2015), p. 22 Goal 12.1; see also para. 28.

[24] UN General Assembly (2015), Transforming our world: the 2030 Agenda for Sustainable Development, G.A. Res. A/RES/70/1 (21 October 2015), p. 22 Goal 12.2.

[25] UN General Assembly (2015), Transforming our world: the 2030 Agenda for Sustainable Development, G.A. Res. A/RES/70/1 (21 October 2015), p. 22 Goal 12.4.

[26] UN General Assembly (2015), Transforming our world: the 2030 Agenda for Sustainable Development, G.A. Res. A/RES/70/1 (21 October 2015), p. 22 Goal 12.5.

[27] Huck (2022), Goal 12 paras. 32 sqq.

[28] Downie and Levy (2000), pp. 355 sqq.

[29] UN (1972), Report of the UN Conference on the human environment, Stockholm, 5–16 June 1972, A/CONF.48/14/Rev. 1 (UN publication, Sales No. E.73.II.A.14), pp. 3 sqq.; see also Sohn (1973), pp. 424 sqq.

[30] UN Environment Programme (2024), UNEP organization chart (22 August 2023).

Intergovernmental Negotiating Committee (INC) on Plastic Pollution.[31] Behind the backdrop of an ever-rising salience, importance, and complexity of Global Environmental Governance (GEG)[32] and multiple global actors addressing a common problem, for instance in conjunction with the UN Industrial Development Organization (UNIDO) under the umbrella of the Global Alliance on Circular Economy and Resource Efficiency (GACERE)[33] and its related initiatives,[34] the Green Growth Knowledge Platform[35] and the Joint UNIDO/UNEP National Cleaner Production Centres (NCPC) Programme,[36] demands for reforms have emerged, notably regarding the establishment of a UN Environment Organization (UNEO), UN Environment Protection Organization (UNEPO) or World Environment Organization (WEO), an international organization with legal personality similar to the World Trade Organization (WTO) or World Health Organization (WHO).[37] Relying on SDG 12, the UNEP works on Sustainable Consumption and Production (SCP) Policies to decouple economic growth from environmental degradation and delivers respective reports, books, booklets, roadmaps and other documents or publications on Single-Use Plastic (SUP) Products,[38] Packaging Policy[39] and Circular Economy.[40]

---

[31] UN Environment Programme (2024), UNEP organization chart (22 August 2023).

[32] Najam et al. (2006), Global Environmental Governance, pp. 9 sqq.; Urho et al. (2019), pp. 23 sqq.; Brown (2012), pp. 125 sqq.

[33] UN Environment Programme (2022), Concept Note – Global Alliance on Circular Economy and Resource Efficiency (GACERE): Towards Just Transitions (July 2022).

[34] UN Environment Programme (2022), Concept Note – Global Alliance on Circular Economy and Resource Efficiency (GACERE): Towards Just Transitions (July 2022), p. 2 names the following global circular economy initiatives: The World Circular Economy Forum (WCEF), the Platform for Accelerating the Circular Economy (PACE), the Partnership for Action on Green Economy (PAGE), and the 10 Year Framework of Programmes on Sustainable Consumption and Production Patterns / One Planet Network (10YFP/OPN).

[35] Citaristi (2022), p. 377; Canton (2021) p. 367; Adamowicz (2022), pp. 5 sq., 14; see also Smith (2010), pp. 251 sq. for the Global Alliance for Clean Cookstoves.

[36] Van Berkel (2011), pp. 161 sqq.; Luken and Navratil (2004), pp. 196 sqq.

[37] Desai (2014), pp. 10f sqq.; Biermann (2015), pp. 182 sqq.; Vijge (2010), pp. 1 sqq.

[38] UN Environment Programme (2022), Single-use Supermarket Food Packaging and its Alternatives: Recommendations from Life Cycle Assessments, Report (1 December 2022); UN Environment Programme (2021), Tackling Plastic Pollution: Legislative Guide for the Regulation of Single-Use Plastic Products, Report (6 April 2021); UN Environment Programme (2020), Single-use Plastic Bags and their Alternatives. Recommendations from Life Cycle Assessments, Report (5 March 2020); UN Environment Programme (2019), New Plastics Economy Global. Commitment 2019 – Progress Report, Report (28 October 2019).

[39] UN Environment Programme (2021), From Pollution to Solution. A Global Assessment of Marine Litter and Plastic Pollution, Report (21 November 2021); UN Environment Programme (2021), Drowning in Plastics. Marine Litter and Plastic Waste Vital Graphics, Report (21 October 2021); UN Environment Programme (2019), Addressing Marine Plastics: A Systemic Approach. Recommendations for Actions, Report (2 December 2019).

[40] UN Environment Programme (2023), Turning off the Tap. How the world can end plastic pollution and create a circular economy, Report (16 May 2023); UN Environment Programme (2023), Chemicals in Plastics. A Technical Report, Report (3 May 2023); UN Environment Programme

2.4 United Nations Environment Assembly

As a result of the 1972 Stockholm Conference,[41] the Governing Council of the UN Environment Programme was established in the same year on the legal basis of Article 22 UNC,[42] which installed in 1985 a subsidiary organ, the so-called Committee of Permanent Representatives, to consider and to make recommandations to the Governing Council.[43] In 2013 the UN General Assembly decided to rename it to UN Environment Assembly (UNEA),[44] following a recommendation of the Governing Council.[45] Since its first session, resulting in a respective resolution,[46] plastics and microplastics in the context of marine litter were a key agenda item at the UNEA[47] and have subsequently remained a topic in further sessions and of consecutive resolutions.[48] During its fourth session, Circular Economy, especially regarding single-use plastic products pollution[49] and innovative pathways to achieve sustainable consumption and production,[50] was held to be a source of innovation, which shall be promoted through relevant meetings and conferences, such as those

(2021), Addressing Single-Use Plastic Products Pollution using a Life Cycle Approach, Report (30 June 2021); UN Environment Programme (2019), The Role of Packaging Regulations and Standards in Driving the Circular Economy, Report (13 November 2019); UN Environment Programme (2019), Addressing Marine Plastics: A Roadmap to a Circular Economy, Roadmap (2019).

41 UN, Report of the UN Conference on the human environment, Stockholm, 5–16 June 1972, A/CONF.48/14/Rev. 1 (UN publication, Sales No. E.73.II.A.14), pp. 29 sqq.

42 UN General Assembly (1972), Institutional and financial arrangements for international environmental cooperation, G.A. Res. A/RES/27/2997 (15 December 1972).

43 Governing Council of the United Nations Environment Programme (1985), Establishment of a Committee of Permanent Representatives, UNEP/GC.13/2 (23 May 1985), Annex, GC Decision 13/2.

44 UN General Assembly (2013), Change of the designation of the Governing Council of the UN Environment Programme, G.A. Res. A/RES/67/251 (25 July 2013).

45 Governing Council of the United Nations Environment Programme (2013), Proceedings of the Governing Council/Global Ministerial Environment Forum at its first universal session, UNEP/GC.27/17 (12 March 2013), Annex I, GC Decision 27/2, para. 1.

46 UN Environment Assembly (2014), Marine plastic debris and microplastics, UNEP/EA.1/Res.6 (2014).

47 UN Environment Assembly (2014), Proceedings of the UN Environment Assembly of the UN Environment Programme at its first session, Nairobi, 23–27 June 2014, UNEP/EA.1/10 (2 September 2014), paras. 64, 70. See also Wendenburg (2019), pp. 88 sqq.; Moses et al. (2019), pp. 93 sqq.

48 UN Environment Assembly (2019), Compilation of UN Environment Assembly resolutions on marine litter and microplastics, Ad hoc open-ended expert group on marine litter and microplastics, third meeting Bangkok, 18–22 November 2019, UNEP/AHEG/2019/3/INF/2 (29 October 2019) with reference to UNEP/EA.1/Res.6; UNEP/EA.2/Res.11; UNEP/EA.3/Res.7; UNEP/EA.4/Res.6.

49 UN Environment Assembly (2019), Addressing single-use plastic products pollution, UNEP/EA.4/Res.9 (28 March 2019).

50 UN Environment Assembly (2019), Innovative pathways to achieve sustainable consumption and production, UNEP/EA.4/Res.1 (28 March 2019).

of the World Circular Economy Forum.[51] The fifth session showed efforts, also resulting in a resolution,[52] towards an international legally binding instrument to end plastic pollution.[53]

2.5 United Nations Plastic Pollution Treaty

The UNEP 50 years anniversary and the resumed fifth session of UNEA (UNEA-5.2) in 2022 mark—due to the declared goal of a UN Plastic Pollution Treaty—a significant event in the history of international policy-making in the field of Packaging Policy and Circular Economy.[54] By adopting the resolution UNEP/EA.5/Res.14[55] the UNEA annouced its ambition to develop an internationally legally binding instrument on plastic pollution, including marine environment, until the end of 2024 and resulting from the work of an Intergovernmental Negotiating Committee (INC).[56] The INC's mandate covers the development of both binding and voluntary approaches, based on a comprehensive approach that addresses the full life cycle of plastic, taking into account, among other factors, the principles of the Rio Declaration on Environment and Development, as well as national circumstances and capabilities, and a catalogue of various further aspects.[57] The negotiations have taken place in alternating places and during different periods, namely in the constellations of the

[51] UN Environment Assembly (2019), Proceedings of the UN Environment Assembly at its fourth session, Nairobi, 11–15 March 2019, UNEP/EA.4/2 (22 March 2019), paras. 58, 66; see in that context also European Commission (2020), Leading the way to a global circular economy: state of play and outlook, Commission Staff Working Document of 11.03.2020, SWD(2020) 100 final, p. 24: "As the world's highest decision making body on the environment, the UN Environment Assembly (UNEA) has an important role in promoting a global circular economy. A EU-supported resolution on the circular economy was adopted at the fourth meeting of the Assembly (UNEA-4), held in Nairobi in March 2019. The resolution on 'Innovative pathways to achieve sustainable consumption and production' acknowledges that a more circular economy can significantly contribute to sustainable consumption and production and invites the UN Member States to consider approaches and policies for achieving sustainable consumption and production, including but not limited to improving resource efficiency and moving towards a circular economy."

[52] UN Environment Assembly (2022), End plastic pollution: towards an international legally binding instrument, UNEP/EA.5/Res.14 (7 March 2022).

[53] UN General Assembly (2022), Report of the UN Environment Assembly of the UN Environment Programme, resumed fifth session, Nairobi, 28 February to 2 March 2022, A/77/25, para. 32; UN General Assembly (2019), UN General Assembly (2019), Proceedings of the UN Environment Assembly at its fourth session, Nairobi, 11–15 March 2019, UNEP/EA.4/2 (22 March 2019), paras. 58, 66.

[54] Stöfen-O'Brien (2022), pp. 377 sqq.; Junankar (2023), pp. 220 sqq.; Bundela and Pandey (2022), pp. 332 sqq.; Denta (2022), pp. 211 sqq.

[55] UN Environment Assembly (2022), End plastic pollution: towards an international legally binding instrument, UNEP/EA.5/Res.14 (7 March 2022).

[56] UN Environment Assembly (2022), End plastic pollution: towards an international legally binding instrument, UNEP/EA.5/Res.14 (7 March 2022), paras. 1, 3.

[57] UN Environment Assembly (2022), End plastic pollution: towards an international legally binding instrument, UNEP/EA.5/Res.14 (7 March 2022), paras. 3 sq.

first session in Punta del Este, Uruguay, from 28th November to 2nd December 2022 (INC-1), the second session in Paris, France, from 29th May to 2nd June 2023 (INC-2), the third session in Nairobi, Kenya, from 13th to 19th November 2023 (INC-3), the fourth session in Ottawa, Canada, from 23rd to 29th April 2024 (INC-4), the first part of the fifth session in Busan, Republic of Korea, from 25th November to 1st December 2024 (INC-5.1), the second part of the fifth session in Geneva, Switzerland, from 5th to 14th August 2025 (INC-5.2), and the third part of the fifth session in Geneva, Switzerland, on 7th February 2026 (INC-5.3). Since an agreement had not been reached within the scheduled time and the UNEA ambition to strike a deal until the end of 2024 had timed out, the bargaining process was extended and the negotiations were scheduled to be resumed in further negotiation sessions in 2025.[58] Despite intensive talks, the Intergovernmental Negotiating Committee has not concluded on a final treaty in 2025 due to deep divisions, especially over production and waste management requirements in the entire chain of production[59] as well as financial mechanisms.[60] Substantive negotiations on the treaty text are expected to resume in subsequent sessions later in 2026, as the international community seeks to bridge the gap between high-ambition targets and the positions of major plastic-producing nations.

[58] UN Environment Programme (2024), Budget overview for the period 2024–2025, UNEP/PP/INC.5/INF/2 (22 November 2024), paras. I.2.b, III.

[59] See UN Environment Programme (2025), Report of the intergovernmental negotiating committee to develop an international legally binding instrument on plastic pollution, including in the marine environment, on the work of its resumed fifth session, UNEP/PP/INC.5/9 (10 September 2025), para. 96.

[60] See UN Environment Programme (2025), Report of the intergovernmental negotiating committee to develop an international legally binding instrument on plastic pollution, including in the marine environment, on the work of its resumed fifth session, UNEP/PP/INC.5/9 (10 September 2025), paras. 38, 79, 99.

European Environmental Governance Actors

3

Abstract

European Packaging Policy and the transition towards a Circular Economy are shaped by a multi-layered system of European Environmental Governance. The relevant institutional actors include the European Commission, the European External Action Service, the European Environment Agency, the European Parliament, and the Council of the European Union. Their respective mandates, competences, and interaction patterns determine agenda-setting, policy formulation, implementation, and external representation. Particular relevance is attributed to the internal differentiation within the European Commission, especially regarding Circular Economy governance and environmental diplomacy, as well as to the EU's role in multilateral environmental fora. Within this framework, Packaging Policy is the outcome of coordinated action in a complex governance network, in which regulatory authority, scientific expertise, political oversight, and external diplomacy are structurally interconnected.

The governance network shaping the European Union's Packaging Policy and Circular Economy landscape includes the European Commission as the primary driver of the legislative agenda and the European Parliament alongside the Council of the European Union as co-legislators responsible for refining and adopting policies. These institutions are supported by the European Environment Agency (EEA) through the provision of critical monitoring and data as well as the European External Action Service (EEAS) through the management of the international dimensions and diplomacy related to these initiatives.

R. H. D. Reimer, *Packaging Policy and Circular Economy*, Law for Professionals, https://doi.org/10.1007/978-3-032-27081-8_3

3.1 European Commission

The European Commission's appearance as a European Environmental Governance Actor can be subdivided into the Circular Economy Directorate and the Green Dipolmacy & Multilateralism Directorate. Within these institutional bodies, the European Commission occupies a structurally central position, as it not only initiates legislative proposals but also internally and externally coordinates policy development across sectors, ensures coherence between environmental and industrial objectives, and shapes the strategic orientation of the Union's Circular Economy transition.

3.1.1 Circular Economy Directorate

The European Commission's Directorate General for Environment (DG ENV) contains the Directorate Circular Economy (DG ENV.B),[1] which is subdivided into four units, namely Circular Economy, Sustainable Production and Consumption (DG ENV.B1), Safe and Sustainable Chemicals (DG ENV.B2), From Waste to Resources (DG ENV.B3), and Sustainable Products (DG ENV.B4), and is supported by an advisor for Circular Economy.[2] The DG ENV follows the European Commission's work programme[3] and structures its work by strategic plans,[4] management plans,[5] and annual activity repots.[6] The DG ENV's Strategic Plan 2020–2024 (Environment) identifies Circular Economy as "Specific Objective 1: The EU economy is more circular and uses natural resources and products more sustainably", refers to its recognition as cornerstone of Europe's new growth strategy in the European Green Deal, and points at the 35 interrelated initiatives[7] of the Circular Economy Action Plan to make products, services, and business models more sustainable, transform consumption patterns, reduce, and transform waste into new resources, in Europe

[1] European Commission (2023), Environment – organisation chart names as other Directorates: General Affairs, Knowledge and Resources (DG ENV.A), Zero Pollution (DG ENV.C), Biodiversity (DG ENV.D), Compliance, Governance & Support to Member States (DG ENV.E) and Green Dipolmacy & Multilateralism (DG ENV.F).

[2] European Commission (2023), Environment – organisation.

[3] See European Commission (2022), Commission work programme 2023. A Union standing firm and united, Communication of 18.10.2022, COM(2022) 548 final.

[4] See European Commission (2020), Strategic plan 2020–2024 – Environment, Ref. Ares(2020)4902415 – 18/09/2020.

[5] See European Commission (2022), Management plan 2022 – Environment, Ref. Ares(2022)342601 – 17/01/2022.

[6] See European Commission (2022), Annual activity report 2021 – Environment, Ref. Ares(2022)2419650 – 31/03/2022.

[7] See also Mhatre et al. (2021), pp. 187 sqq.

and beyond.[8] Sustainable Product Policy[9] and key value chains waste streams,[10] especially concerning plastics, are directly addressed in the document. According to its annex, which contains policy performance tables, the number of EU Ecolabel products,[11] the eco-innovation index,[12] the municipal waste generation and treatment,[13] the export of waste outside the EU,[14] and the proportion of proposed legislative revisions that include burden reduction measures[15] are the relevant result indicators[16] to measure the policy outcome[17] in specific objective 1 „Circular Economy“.[18]

3.1.2 Green Diplomacy & Multilateralism Directorate

Behind the backdrop of its competences, the European Commission can be considered as major actor in the EU's external relations in environmental policy.[19] It exerts its powers in terms of an external dimension as a global actor through its Directorate Green Dipolmacy & Multilateralism (DG ENV.F)[20] and a common concept, namely its Global Circular Economy Policy, which characterizes especially the following policy approaches:

The European Commission advocates on behalf of the EU for the Global Alliance on Circular Economy and Resource Efficiency (GACERE) in conjunction with UNEP and UNIDO to implement the UN 2030 Agenda Sustainable Development Goals[21] and claims to take over leadership, promoting the role of the EU as a global

---

8 See European Commission (2020), Strategic plan 2020-2024 – Environment, Ref. Ares(2020)4902415 – 18/09/2020, p. 8.

9 See European Commission (2020), Strategic plan 2020–2024 – Environment, Ref. Ares(2020)4902415 – 18/09/2020, pp. 8 sqq.

10 See European Commission (2020), Strategic plan 2020-2024 – Environment, Ref. Ares(2020)4902415 – 18/09/2020, pp. 10 sqq.

11 Result indicator 1.1.

12 Result indicator 1.2.

13 Result indicator 1.3.

14 Result indicator 1.4.

15 Result indicator 1.5.

16 See also Moraga et al. (2019), pp. 452; Völker et al. (2020), pp. 103 sqq.

17 See also Mazur-Wierzbicka (2021), pp. 1 sqq.

18 See European Commission (2020), Strategic plan 2020–2024 – Environment, Ref. Ares(2020)4902415 – 18/09/2020, p. 38 sq.

19 Spence (2004), pp. 62 sqq.

20 European Commission (2023), Environment – organisation chart.

21 UN Environment Programme (2022), Concept Note – Global Alliance on Circular Economy and Resource Efficiency (GACERE): Towards Just Transitions (July 2022); European Commission (2020), A New Circular Economy Action Plan. For a cleaner and more competitive Europe, Communication of 11.3.2020, COM(2020) 98 final, p. 3.

leader.[22] The Global Circular Economy Alliance is set out to identify knowledge and governance gaps in advancing global circular economy and take forward partnership initiatives, including with major economies, as well as a tool to support the Circular Economy transition through multilateral fora, such as the G7 or G20.[23] Aknowledging that the environmental ambition of the Green Deal will not be achieved by Europe acting alone,[24] the European Commission aims to mobilize its neighbours and partners to join it on a sustainable path and wants to build alliances with the like-minded.[25] Circular Economy shall work for people, regions, and cities, fully contribute to climate neutrality, and harnesses the potential of research, innovation, and digitalisation[26] by bringing together other global champions of Circular Economy and sustainable resource management including relevant international organisations and bodies, selected partner countries and regions, business associations, NGOs, and academia.[27] Addressing the work on the UN Plastic Pollution Treaty, the European Commission considers the very low reuse and recycling of end-of-life plastics, compared to other material streams and due to the cheap price of plastics, as problematic,[28] while it supports international action, promotes best practices worldwide, and uses its external funding instruments to support improved waste prevention and management around the world.[29] Furthermore, the European Commission also applies policy dialogues on environment and industry and on dialogues under free trade agreements as external policy tools in Packaging Policy and Circular Economy matters.[30]

---

[22] European Commission (2019), The European Green Deal, Communication of 11.12.2019, COM(2019) 640 final, pp. 20 sqq.; A New Circular Economy Action Plan. For a cleaner and more competitive Europe, Communication of 11.3.2020, COM(2020) 98 final, pp. 3, 18 sq.; Report on the implementation of the Circular Economy Action Plan, Report of 4.3.2019, COM(2019) 190 final, p. 7.

[23] European Commission (2020), Leading the way to a global circular economy: state of play and outlook, Commission Staff Working Dokument of 11.03.2020, SWD(2020) 100 final, p. 20.

[24] European Commission (2019), The European Green Deal, Communication of 11.12.2019, COM(2019) 640 final, p. 2; European Commission (2020), A New Circular Economy Action Plan. For a cleaner and more competitive Europe, Communication of 11.3.2020, COM(2020) 98 final, p. 3.

[25] European Commission (2019), The European Green Deal, Communication of 11.12.2019, COM(2019) 640 final, p. 2.

[26] European Commission (2020), A New Circular Economy Action Plan. For a cleaner and more competitive Europe, Communication of 11.3.2020, COM(2020) 98 final, p. 3.

[27] European Commission (2020), Leading the way to a global circular economy: state of play and outlook, Commission Staff Working Dokument of 11.03.2020, SWD(2020) 100 final, p. 20.

[28] European Commission (2020), Leading the way to a global circular economy: state of play and outlook, Commission Staff Working Dokument of 11.03.2020, SWD(2020) 100 final, pp. 20 sq.

[29] European Commission (2018), A European Strategy for Plastics in a Circular Economy, Communication of 16.1.2018, COM(2018) 28 final, p. 16.

[30] European Commission (2018), A European Strategy for Plastics in a Circular Economy, Communication of 16.1.2018, COM(2018) 28 final, p. 16.

3.2 European External Action Service

The European Commission's Global Circular Economy Policy is not the only European voice on Packaging Policy and Circular Economy in the global arena. The European External Action Service (EEAS) is another global actor, who promotes its Climate, Environment & Energy Diplomacy in the EU's External Relations. The EEAS works on Circular Economy within its environment policy,[31] which is a part of its Climate, Environment & Energy Diplomacy.[32] According to the European Commission the EEAS plays a key role in facilitating the Circular Economy transition in third countries, notably in the context of the "Green Deal Diplomacy[33]", as well as through bilateral cooperation, because EU delegations can make use of the synergies with the EU's Climate Diplomacy and with their knowledge of the EU's policy priorities for the country, the local conditions, policy dynamics, and activities by EU Member States and European businesses, in order to encourage the adoption of energy and resource-efficient, low carbon and circular growth models suitable for the local conditions.[34] International cooperations, such as the EU-India Partnership for Circular Economy and Resource Efficiency[35] or the EU-Gulf Cooperation Council (GCC) Dialogue on Economic Diversification,[36] are a major tool to effectuate the EEAS's Climate, Environment & Energy Diplomacy in the global arena.

3.3 European Environment Agency

The European Environment Agency (EEA)[37] and its European Environment Information and Observation Network (Eionet),[38] which are based on Article 1 para. 1 Regulation (EC) No 401/2009, are important think tanks for Packaging Policy and Circular Economy and provide according to Article 1 para. 2 Regulation (EC) No 401/2009 the EU and the Member States with objective, reliable and comparable information and the necessary technical and scientific support. While Article 2 lit. a

[31] Woolcock (2012), pp. 117 sqq.; Hadfield and Fiott (2014), pp. 173 sq.

[32] Torney and Davis Cross (2018), pp.39 sqq.; Burns and Tobin (2018), p. 325; Kern et al. (2020), p. 182.

[33] European Commission (2019), The European Green Deal, Communication of 11.12.2019, COM(2019) 640 final, pp. 20 sqq.

[34] European Commission (2020), Leading the way to a global circular economy: state of play and outlook, Commission Staff Working Dokument of 11.03.2020, SWD(2020) 100 final, pp. 35 sq.

[35] European External Action Service (2020), EU-India: Partners for Circular Economy & Resource Efficiency, Broschure of 28.09.2020.

[36] European External Action Service (2021), EU-Gulf Cooperation Council (GCC) Dialogue on Economic Diversification. Gulf Cooperation Council (GCC) Countries. Study on Circular Economy developments in the GCC region and opportunities for collaboration with the European Union, Report of 1.4.2021.

[37] See also Dammann and Gee (2011), pp. 238 sqq.; Martens (2010), pp. 881 sqq.; Caspersen (1999), pp. 71 sqq.

[38] See also Hřebíček (2003), pp. 65 sqq.; Heussner (2007), pp. 62 sqq.; Schwind (2017), pp. 170 sqq.

to o Regulation (EC) No 401/2009 lists the various tasks of the agency, Article 3 para. 2 Regulation (EC) No 401/2009 names different work area priorities, comprising especially waste management in Article 3 para. 2 lit. e Regulation (EC) No 401/2009. According to Article 4 para. 1 Regulation (EC) No 401/2009 Eionet is composed of the main component elements of the national information networks,[39] national focal points[40] and topic centres.[41]

The EEA has delivered several publications on Packaging Policy and Circular Economy, such as conditions and pathways for sustainable and circular consumption in Europe,[42] pathways towards circular plastics in Europe,[43] tracking waste prevention progress,[44] investigating Europe's secondary raw material markets,[45] resource efficiency and the circular economy in Europe 2019,[46] paving the way for a circular economy,[47] biodegradable and compostable plastics,[48] the plastic waste trade in the circular economy,[49] plastics, the circular economy and Europe's environment,[50] and preventing plastic waste in Europe.[51]

The Eionet encompasses the European Topic Centre on Circular Economy and Resource Use (ETC CE), which was designed as a consortium from 2022 to 2026 under the lead of the Vlaamse Instelling voor Technologish Onderzoek (VITO), bringing together 13 partner organisations[52] that profit from the mutual knowledge

---

[39] Article 4 para. 1 lit. a Regulation (EC) No 401/2009.

[40] Article 4 para. 1 lit. b Regulation (EC) No 401/2009.

[41] Article 4 para. 1 lit. c Regulation (EC) No 401/2009.

[42] European Environment Agency (2023), Conditions and pathways for sustainable and circular consumption in Europe, Report of 13.6.2023.

[43] European Environment Agency (2023), Pathways towards circular plastics in Europe – good practice examples from countries, business and citizens, Report of 20.2.2023.

[44] European Environment Agency (2023), Tracking waste prevention progress – A narrative-based waste prevention monitoring framework at the EU level, Report No 2/2023 of 17.5.2023.

[45] European Environment Agency (2023), Investigating Europe's secondary raw material markets, Report No 12/2022 of 26.1.2023.

[46] European Environment Agency (2020), Resource efficiency and the circular economy in Europe 2019 – even more from less. An overview of the policies, approaches and targets of 32 European countries, Report No 26/2019 of 1.4.2020.

[47] European Environment Agency (2019), Paving the way for a circular economy: insights on status and potentials, Report No 11/2019 of 1.10.2019.

[48] European Environment Agency (2020), Biodegradable and compostable plastics – challenges and opportunities, Report of 27.8.2020.

[49] European Environment Agency (2020), The plastic waste trade in the circular economy, Report of 28.10.2020.

[50] European Environment Agency (2021), Plastics, the circular economy and Europe's environment – A priority for action, Report No 18/2020 of 28.1.2021.

[51] European Environment Agency (2019), Preventing plastic waste in Europe, Report No 2/2019 of 3.6.2019.

[52] The 12 partner organisations coordinated by VITO are Banson Editorial and Communications Ltd (BEC), Czech Environmental Information Agency (CENIA)/Česká informační agentura životního prostředí, Collaborating Centre on Sustainable Consumption and Production (CSCP), Research Institute on Sustainable Economic Growth of the National Research Council of Italy/

and exchange. Among other works, the ETC CE has published reports on the fate of EU plastic waste,[53] pathways to circular plastics in Europe,[54] analysis of the circular material use rate and the doubling target,[55] and flexible plastics in Europe's circular economy.[56]

3.4 European Parliament

The European Parliament appears as European Environmental Governance Actor through its Committee on the Environment, Public Health, and Food Safety and the European Parliamentary Research Service.

3.4.1 Committee on the Environment, Public Health and Food Safety

In accordance with Rule 57 para. 1 PRP and Annex VIII para. 1 lit. b[57] and c[58] European Parliement's Rules of Procedure (PRP) the European Parliament's Committee on the Environment, Public Health and Food Safety (ENVI) has several times been appointed as the responsible parliamentary committee for Circular Economy and Packaging Policy.[59] The ENVI has published several notable (draft) reports, especially on the New CEAP,[60] on the PPWR,[61] on the proposal for a

Istituto di Ricerca sulla Crescita Economica Sostenibile del Consiglio Nazionale delle Ricerche (IRCrES), IVL Swedish Environmental Research Institute/IVL Svenska Miljöinstitutet, PlanMiljø, Sustainable Environmental Economics and Dynamics Studies (SEEDS), German Environment Agency/Umweltbundesamt (UBA), Technical Research Centre of Finland (VTT)/Teknologian tutkimuskeskus VTT Oy, Wuppertal Institut (WI), and World Resources Forum Association (WRFA).

[53] European Topic Centre on Circular Economy and Resource Use (2023), The fate of EU plastic waste, Report 2023/2 of 20.2.2023.

[54] European Topic Centre on Circular Economy and Resource Use (2023), Pathways to circular plastics in Europe: Good examples from countries, business and citizens, Report 2023/1 of 20.2.2023.

[55] European Topic Centre on Circular Economy and Resource Use (2023), Analysis of the circular material use rate and the doubling target, Report 2023/6 of 25.4.2023.

[56] European Topic Centre on Circular Economy and Resource Use (2022), Flexible plastics in Europe's circular economy, Report 4/2022 of 28.9.2022.

[57] I.e., "waste management and recycling".

[58] I.e., "sustainable development".

[59] See also European Parliament (2022), Resource efficiency and circular economy, Fact sheet of 1.9.2022, pp. 5 sq.

[60] European Parliament (2021), Report on the New Circular Economy Action Plan of 28.1.2021, 2020/2077(INI), A9-0008/2021, PE652.387v03-00.

[61] European Parliament (2023), Draft report on on the proposal for a regulation of the European Parliament and of the Council on packaging and packaging waste, amending Regulation (EU) 2019/1020 and Directive (EU) 2019/904, and repealing Directive 94/62/EC of 11.4.2023, COM(2022)0677, C9-0400/2022, 2022/0396(COD), PE742.297v01-00.

regulation of the European Parliament and of the Council amending the CLPR,[62] and other related policy areas.

3.4.2 European Parliamentary Research Service

The European Parliamentary Research Service (EPRS) is a directorate general of the European Parliament, which provides the latter with research and expertise to ensure the parliament's independent access to information.[63] Among other publications, the EPRS, namely its Panel for the Future of Science and Technology (STOA), has delivered a comprehensive study on Circular Economy,[64] that specifically addresses the field of Packaging Policy[65] and Single-Use Plastics in the context of the European Green Deal.[66] The EPRS has considered Circular Economy also as a part of the EU climate action policy.[67] In the context of Packaging Policy, the EPRS also published a briefing concerning the revision of the PPWD, which is within the responsibility of the European Parliament's Committee on Environment, Public Health, and Food Safety for the PPWR.[68]

3.5 Council of the European Union

The Council of the European Union exerts its influence as European Environmental Governance Actor on the basis of the Council of the European Union's Rules of Procedure (CRP) through its various configurations in the sense of Article 16 para. 6 TEU, Article 236 lit. a TFEU, especially via the Environment Council (ENV) in the field of Packaging Policy and Circular Economy.[69] Although the Council, as

[62] European Parliament (2023), Draft Report on the proposal for a regulation of the European Parliament and of the Council amending Regulation (EC) No 1272/2008 of the European Parliament and of the Council on classification, labelling and packaging of substances and mixtures of 5.4.2023, COM(2022)0748, C9-0433/2022, 2022/0432(COD), PE745.493v01-00.

[63] Ripoll Servant (2018), pp. 178 sq.; Hilbert (2022), pp. 331 sq.

[64] European Parliamentary Research Service (2017), Towards a circular economy – Waste management in the EU, Study PE 581.913 of 25.9.2017.

[65] European Parliamentary Research Service (2017), Towards a circular economy – Waste management in the EU, Study PE 581.913 of 25.9.2017, pp. 25 sq., 42 sqq., 67 sqq.

[66] European Parliamentary Research Service (2022), The Green Deal ambition: Technology, creativity and the arts for environmental sustainability, Study PE 729.513 of 31.5.2022, p. 42; European Parliamentary Research Service (2021), Meeting the Green Deal objectives by alignment of technology and behaviour, Study PE 656.337 of 9.7.2021, p. 28.

[67] European Parliamentary Research Service (2021), EU climate action policy: Responding to the global emergency, Study PE 689.378 of 18.3.2021.

[68] European Parliamentary Research Service (2023), Revision of the Packaging and Packaging Waste Directive, Briefing PE 745.707 of 31.3.2023.

[69] See Tömmel (2014), pp. 95 sq.; Ginsberg (2010), pp. 158 sq.; Lewis (2007), pp. 155 sqq.; Nedergard (2007), pp. 142 sqq.; Hayes-Renshaw and Wallace (2006), pp. 33 sqq.

competent institution, takes the final decisions in the law-making process, it is assisted by its preparatory bodies. The Committee of Permanent Representatives/ Comité des représentants permanents (COREPER), which is devided into the deputy heads of mission predominantely dealing with socio-economic questions under the support of the so-called preparatory Mertens Group (COREPER I) and the heads of mission dealing mainly with judicial, domestic, financial, and foreign affairs under the support of the so-called preparatory Antici Group (COREPER II), backs in accordance with Article 16 para. 7 TEU, Article 240 para. 1 TFEU, Article 19 CRP the Council by the endorsement of interinstitutional agreements, by the formulation of Council conclusions, and by fulfilling other tasks.[70] According to Article 19 para. 3 CRP, futher preparatory work may be delegated to the Committees or Working Parties appointed by the General Secretariat (GSC).[71] In addition to the deliberations from these preparatory bodies, the Genreal Secretariat assists the Council through its different directorates, their units, their sectors, and their offices, in the area of Packaging Policy and Circular Economy especially by the work delivered by the directorate Environment, Education, Transport, Telecom and Energy (TREE), its unit Environment, Education, Youth, Culture, Audiovisual and Sport (TREE.1) and the aforementioned unit's sector Environment and Climate Change (TREE.1.A).[72]

[70] See Lewis (2022), pp. 323 sqq.; Ginsberg (2010), pp. 159 sq.; Tömmel (2014), pp. 96 sq.; Lewis (2007), pp. 164 sq.; Nedergard (2007), pp. 156 sqq.; Hayes-Renshaw and Wallace (2006), pp. 72 sqq.

[71] See Tömmel (2014), pp. 97 sq.; Ginsberg (2010), p. 160; Lewis (2007), pp. 165 sq.; Nedergard (2007), pp. 160 sqq.; Hayes-Renshaw and Wallace (2006), pp. 82 sqq., 96 sqq.

[72] Council of the European Council (2025), General Secretariat of the Council (GSC) organisation chart (16 January 2025).

European Packaging Legislation

4

Abstract

European Packaging Legislation rests on a determining legal basis within the EU Treaties and is guided by fundamental principles of European environmental and waste law. Its regulatory architecture combines internal market integration with environmental protection through a differentiated and interlinked system, which lends coherence to the regulatory framework aligning policy objectives, ensuring legal convergence across Member States, and anchoring packaging legislation within the broader structure of EU waste law. Central mechanisms of the European Packaging Legislation include the waste hierarchy, regulatory bans, material and design requirements, quantitative targets, information obligations, and Extended Producer Responsibility schemes. These instruments do not operate in isolation, but are structured and coordinated through the regulatory system, which ensures coherence between environmental objectives and internal market functioning in a Circular Economy. This legal framework thus lays down normative principles for operational rules that structure market behaviour, allocate responsibility, and promote resource efficiency across the entire life cycle of packaging within a system of interconnected governance mechanisms.

European packaging legislation forms the normative core through which the objectives of Circular Economy policy are translated into binding legal structures. It is within this legal framework that political ambitions are transformed into concrete obligations, regulatory standards, and enforceable mechanisms that shape the conduct of economic actors across the packaging value chain. The following section therefore turns to the legal basis, guiding principles, regulatory architecture, and policy instruments that collectively define how European law structures and stabilizes the transition towards more resource-efficient and sustainable packaging systems.

R. H. D. Reimer, *Packaging Policy and Circular Economy*, Law for Professionals, https://doi.org/10.1007/978-3-032-27081-8_4

4.1 Legal Basis

Packaging Policy and Circular Economy are a cross-sectional matter of economical and environmental questions. According to Article 11 TFEU, Packaging Policy and Circular Economy, in their function as environmental protection requirements, must be integrated into the definition and implementation of the EU's policies and activities, in particular with a view to promoting sustainable development. Hence, secondary legal actions under Article 288 TFEU, namely predominantly regulations and directives, in that policy field rely either on Article 114 TFEU (internal market) or on Article 191 para. 1 TFEU (environment) as legal basis. In that conext, a clear distinction between the applicable primary law competence is mandatory. That is not only because of the principle of conferral[1] and its related, competence-limiting principles of susbsidiarity and proportionality,[2] but also against the backdrop of the exclusive and shared competences system of Article 2 to 6 TFEU. While policies relating to the internal market[3] or the environment[4] are generally shared competences and as such subject to the restrictions of Article 2 para. 2 to 6 TFEU, they might in a particular case even be in the scope of the EU's exclusive competences for the establishing of the competition rules necessary for the functioning of the internal market[5] or the conservation of marine biological resources under the common fisheries policy[6] and thus be governed by Article 2 para. 1 TFEU. Furthermore, environmental aspects are regulated differently in Article 114 para. 3 TFEU than in Article 191 para. 2 sentence 1 TFEU. However, a strict distinction between the legal bases will in practice often be unproblematic since each competence of the EU must be interpreted according to the principles of implied powers and *effet utile*. For problematic cases remains otherwise the provision of Article 352 TFEU.[7] In practice, the documents of the EU make a heterogenous appearance. While for example the EU relies for its packaging legislation—which is also within the competence of the European Parliament's Committee on the Environment, Public Health, and Food

[1] Article 5 TEU.

[2] Article 5 para. 1 sentence 2 TEU.

[3] Article 4 para. 2 lit. a TFEU.

[4] Article 4 para. 2 lit. e TFEU.

[5] Article 3 para. 1 lit. b TFEU.

[6] Article 3 para. 1 lit. d TFEU.

[7] See also Streinz (2018), Art. 5 EUV para. 13; Calliess (2022a), Art. 5 EUV paras. 2 sqq.; Vedder (2018), Art. 5 EUV paras. 1 sqq.; Epiney (2019), ch. 5 paras. 5 sqq.

Safety[8]—on Article 114 TFEU (internal market),[9] it refers to Article 191 para. 1 TFEU (environment) in matters of its single-use plastics legislation.[10]

4.2 Basic Principles

The four[11] basic principles of European primary environmental law, which are also applicable to Packaging Policy and Circular Economy, derive from Article 191 para. 2 subpara. 1 sentence 2 TFEU: The precautionary principle, the prevention principle, the rectification at source principle, and the polluter pays principle.[12] These principles determine Packaging Policy and Circular Economy in the EU in a way, that risks or dangers for the environment must be prevented and managed at the early stage of their source, while ensuring the individual responsibility of polluters. The environmental principles of Article 191 para. 2 subpara. 1 sentence 2 TFEU have to be seen in conjunction with the environmental principles of integration and sustainability, which are enshrined in Article 11 TFEU and Article 37 CFR.[13] These norms[14] are neither legal rules nor do they simply pronounce a political agenda, but they are binding legal principles, which inherently call for proportional balancing and equilibration with other principles and optimization against other conflicting interests.[15]

[8] European Parliament (2023), Rule 57 para. 1 and Annex VIII para. 1 lit. b (waste management and recycling) and c (sustainable development) PRP.

[9] European Commission (2022), Proposal for a Regulation of the European Parliament and of the Council on packaging and packaging waste, amending Regulation (EU) 2019/1020 and Directive (EU) 2019/904, and repealing Directive 94/62/EC of 30.11.2022, COM(2022) 677 final, pp. 3 sq.

[10] Directive (EU) 2019/904 of the European Parliament and of the Council of 5 June 2019 on the reduction of the impact of certain plastic products on the environment, OJ L 155, 12.6.2019, p. 1. See also European Commission (2022), Proposal for a Directive of the European Parliament and of the Council concerning urban wastewater treatment (recast) of 26.10.2022, COM(2022) 541 final, p. 5.

[11] See for further principles Kahl (2018), Art. 191 AEUV paras. 103 sqq.; Kloepfer (2016), § 4 para. 2; Kahl and Gärditz (2021), § 4 para. 21.

[12] See also Kahl (2018), Art. 191 AEUV, paras. 72 sqq.; Calliess (2022b), Art. 191 AEUV paras. 16 sqq.; Epiney (2018), Art. 191 AEUV paras. 6 sqq.; Käller (2019), Art. 191 AEUV paras. 25 sqq.; Krämer (2015), Art. 191 AEUV paras. 25 sqq.; Kahl and Gärditz (2021), § 2 paras. 12 sqq., § 4 paras. 21 sqq.

[13] Krämer (2012), p. 85; Kahl and Gärditz (2021), § 2 para. 12; Calliess and Tuncel (2023), pp. 10 sqq., 16 sq.

[14] Kahl (2018), Art. 191 AEUV, art. 191 AEUV paras. 18 sqq.; Proelss (2016), pp. 30 sq.; Scotford (2017), pp. 59 sqq.; Kahl and Gärditz (2021), § 2 paras. 12 sq.; Kozień (2021), pp. 12 sqq.

[15] See for the distinction between rules and principles Neves (2021), pp. 10 sqq.; Peno (2019), pp. 424 sq.; Sieckmann (2011), pp. 178 sqq.; Reßing (2009), pp. 28 sqq.; Borgmann-Prebil (2008), pp. 339 sq.

4.3 Regulatory System

The regulatory system of European Packaging Policy is shaped by a multi-layered interaction between general Circular Economy law and sector-specific packaging regulation. It reflects a deliberately structured legal architecture in which overarching sustainability objectives, foundational principles, and governance mechanisms are developed at the level of general framework legislation and subsequently specified through targeted regulatory regimes. Packaging law operates within this system as a specialised legal field that both derives from and contributes to the broader Circular Economy framework. Its regulatory logic is characterised by policy alignment, legal convergence, and institutional interlinkages, with the Waste Framework Directive functioning as the central normative reference point. This embedded structure ensures coherence across legal spheres while allowing for differentiated regulatory responses to the specific environmental, economic, and functional characteristics of packaging and packaging waste.

4.3.1 Policy Alignment

The interaction between Circular Economy law and Packaging law is characterised by mutual reinforcement. General Circular Economy norms gain practical relevance through sector-specific implementation, while Packaging law derives its legitimacy and coherence from its alignment with general principles. This interaction is particularly evident in areas such as eco-design, market surveillance, and secondary raw materials, where packaging-specific rules operate within a broader regulatory system. European Packaging Policy is thus not an isolated regulatory field, but forms a constitutive component of the European Union's Circular Economy legal framework. Its legal systematic is characterised by an embedded structure in which sector-specific packaging legislation is integrated into a broader body of general Circular Economy law. This framework aims at transforming traditional linear economic models into circular systems that preserve resources, minimise waste generation, and promote material recovery. Circular Economy law functions as a horizontal and cross-sectoral regulatory sphere. It establishes general objectives, principles, and governance mechanisms applicable to a wide range of products, materials, and waste streams. Packaging law, by contrast, operates as a vertical regulatory regime that addresses a clearly defined material flow with distinct environmental, economic, and logistical characteristics. The resulting legal architecture reflects a deliberate differentiation between general framework norms and specialised implementing rules. Within this structure, Packaging Policy performs a dual role. It serves as an instrument for achieving overarching Circular Economy objectives while simultaneously responding to the specific challenges posed by packaging, such as high turnover rates, short use phases, and strong links to consumer behaviour and internal market dynamics. This duality explains both the necessity and the intensity of sector-specific regulation in the field of packaging.

4.3.2 Legal Convergence

The regulatory system of European Packaging Policy is defined by its structural dependence on Circular Economy law and by its function as a specialised instrument for achieving general sustainability objectives. The basic legal framework of the Waste Framework Directive provides the unifying normative structure in this context that ensures conceptual clarity, legal certainty, and regulatory continuity across waste streams. Packaging law complements this structure by delivering the necessary specificity to address a material flow of exceptional environmental and economic importance. The effectiveness of European Packaging Policy ultimately depends on the consistency and coherence between general Circular Economy norms and sector-specific packaging regulation. The regulatory system therefore exemplifies the EU's broader approach to environmental governance, combining general framework legislation with targeted, highly developed special regimes in order to achieve systemic transformation. Against this backdrop, Circular Economy law and Packaging law generally follow the classical legal doctrine of *lex generalis* and *lex specialis*. Circular Economy law constitutes the general normative framework that governs waste prevention, waste management, resource efficiency, and the closing of material cycles across the economy. Packaging law operates as a specialised subset within this framework, refining and concretising general norms for a particular category of products and waste. The *lex generalis* establishes the secondary law outline of fundamental concepts such as waste, recycling, recovery, and disposal, as well as core principles including the waste hierarchy and Extended Producer Responsibility (EPR). These concepts and principles apply across all waste streams unless explicitly modified or specified by sectoral legislation. Packaging law, as *lex specialis*, does not depart from these foundations but rather adapts them to the functional realities of packaging markets and packaging waste systems. This legal relationship ensures both unity and differentiation. Unity is achieved through the uniform application of general Circular Economy principles, while differentiation enables tailored regulatory solutions that address sector-specific risks and opportunities. Packaging law thus represents neither an autonomous legal regime nor a mere technical annex, but a structurally integrated special regime that enhances the effectiveness of Circular Economy law as a whole.

4.3.3 Waste Framework Directive

At the centre of European Circular Economy law stands the Waste Framework Directive[16] (WFD). It provides the conceptual, normative, and structural foundation upon which all sector-specific waste legislation, including packaging law, is built.

[16] Directive 2008/98/EC of the European Parliament and of the Council of 19 November 2008 on waste and repealing certain Directives, OJ L 312, 22.11.2008, p. 3, last amended by Directive (EU) 2025/1892 of the European Parliament and of the Council of 10 September 2025 amending Directive 2008/98/EC on waste, OJ L 2025/1982, 26.9.2025.

Its role extends beyond that of a coordinating instrument and qualifies it as the normative backbone of the European waste and Circular Economy regulatory system. The Waste Framework Directive establishes a uniform definition of waste that is decisive for determining the scope of packaging regulation. Whether packaging materials fall within or outside the waste regime depends on this definition and on the related concepts of by-products and end-of-waste status. These classifications are of particular relevance for packaging, given the economic importance of recycled materials and the objective of reintroducing secondary raw materials into production cycles. The end-of-waste provisions enable packaging materials to exit the waste regime once defined quality and safety criteria are fulfilled, thereby supporting the development of secondary materials markets. In addition, the Waste Framework Directive codifies the waste hierarchy as a legally binding ordering principle. This hierarchy functions as a normative compass for all packaging related regulatory measures. Obligations concerning packaging minimisation, reuse systems, recyclability requirements, and recycled content thresholds derive their legal justification from the hierarchy's prioritisation of prevention and recycling over disposal. Packaging law translates this abstract hierarchy into concrete, enforceable product and market rules, ensuring its practical effectiveness.

4.3.4 Interlinked Governence Mechanisms

A central element of the Waste Framework Directive lies in its governance mechanisms, particularly the establishment of Extended Producer Responsibility (EPR) as a core instrument of Circular Economy law. By shifting responsibility for post-consumer waste management to producers, the Directive operationalizes the polluter pays principle and creates economic incentives for sustainable product design. Packaging law builds upon this governance model and develops it into one of the most comprehensive producer responsibility regimes within European environmental law. It specifies detailed obligations regarding registration, financing, reporting, and organisational structures, thereby transforming the general EPR concept into a highly operational regulatory system. This specification illustrates the function of Packaging law as *lex specialis*, giving concrete form to the general governance logic of the Waste Framework Directive. Beyond producer responsibility, the Directive also provides a horizontal framework for waste management planning, data collection, monitoring, and enforcement. Packaging law relies on this framework to ensure consistency with other waste streams and to avoid regulatory fragmentation. The Waste Framework Directive thus performs a coordinating function that stabilises the overall regulatory system and safeguards its internal coherence.

4.4 Policy Instruments

The EU has developed serevral policy instruments to integrate and transfer its political agenda on the basis of the primary law environmental principles of Article 191 para. 2 subpara. 1 sentence 2 TFEU into secondary law. These tools encompass in particular the waste hierarchy, bans, requirements, targets, information, and extended producer responsibility.

4.4.1 Waste Hierarchy

The waste hierarchy relates to the precautionary principle, the prevention principle, and the rectification at source principle. It is enshrined in Article 4 WFD and prioritizes, hierarchical to the following denomination, the prevention, reuse, recycling, recovery, and disposal of waste. Besides this general provision on waste hierarchy, there are also special waste hierarchy provisions for certain policy areas,[17] such as the former Article 1 para. 2 PPWD[18] in Packaging Policy. A major challenge in that context is the precise synchronization and correct determinition of the applicable law between *lex generalis* and *lex specialis* and among the different levels of a certain waste hierarchy. Article 4 para. 2 subpara. 1 WFD adds to this legal complexity a sphere of practical difficulties, because it governs that, when applying the waste hierarchy referred to in Article 4 para. 1 WFD, Member States shall take measures to encourage the options that deliver the best overall environmental outcome, which may require specific waste streams departing from the hierarchy, where this is justified by life cycle thinking on the overall impacts of the generation and management of such waste.[19] Although Article 4 para. 3 WFD refers to Annex IVa WFD, which contains a catalogue of examples of economic instruments and other measures to provide incentives for the application of the waste hierarchy, it does not shed any light on the qualification of each incentive according to the different levels of the waste hierarchy.

The packaging waste hierarchy of Article 1 para. 2 PPWD correlated formerly with the subsequent Articles 4 to 6 PPWD, which contained further requirements on prevention, reuse, recovery, and recycling, and is now addressed by Article 1 para. 3 PPWR. It can also be interpreted as a guiding principle for the application

[17] See also Reimer (2022), pp. 166 sq.

[18] European Parliament and Council Directive 94/62/EC of 20 December 1994 on packaging and packaging waste, OJ L 365, 31.12.1994, p. 10, last amended by Directive (EU) 2018/852 of the European Parliament and of the Council of 30 May 2018 amending Directive 94/62/EC on packaging and packaging waste, OJ L 150, 14.6.2018, p. 141: "To that end, this Directive lays down measures aimed, as a first priority, at preventing the production of packaging waste and, as additional fundamental principles, at reusing packaging, at recycling and other forms of recovering packaging waste and, therefore, at reducing the final disposal of such waste in order to contribute to the transition towards a circular economy."

[19] See in that context also Olatayo et al. (2022), pp. 1 sqq.; Pires and Martinho (2019), pp. 298 sqq.; Van Ewijk and Stegemann (2016), pp. 122 sqq.; Gharfalkar et al. (2015), pp. 305 sqq.

of—especially Articles 4 to 6 of—the SUPD, since Article 1 SUPD declares to aim to prevent and reduce the impact of certain plastic products on the environment and to promote the transition to a Circular Economy in contribution to the efficient functioning of the internal market. Even more clear, Rec. 10 sentence 1 SUPD states that this directive is a *lex specialis* in relation to the PPWD and the WFD, while this conclusion can already be drawn from Rec. 2 sentences 1 and 2 SUPD, which formulate that the directive promotes circular approaches aiming first and foremost to reduce the quantity of waste generated and that waste prevention is at the pinnacle of the waste hierarchy enshrined in the WFD.

4.4.2 Bans

One of the probably most strict EU's policy tools are bans. Neither the WFD nor the PPWD[20] rely largely[21] on bans. In contrast and in comparison to these established and repeatedly amended legal frameworks, the SUPD is, at least partially, an example of a rather prohibitionist policy. That concerns foremost the market placing restrictions of Article 5 SUPD for the single-use plastics products in part B[22] of the Annex and products made from oxo-degradable plastic, which are, in the light of Rec. 15 sentence 1 SUPD, considered as necessary to achieve the transition to suitable and more sustainable alternatives for certain single-use plastic products.

[20] European Parliament and Council Directive 94/62/EC of 20 December 1994 on packaging and packaging waste, OJ L 365, 31.12.1994, p. 10, last amended by Directive (EU) 2018/852 of the European Parliament and of the Council of 30 May 2018 amending Directive 94/62/EC on packaging and packaging waste, OJ L 150, 14.6.2018, p. 141: "To that end, this Directive lays down measures aimed, as a first priority, at preventing the production of packaging waste and, as additional fundamental principles, at reusing packaging, at recycling and other forms of recovering packaging waste and, therefore, at reducing the final disposal of such waste in order to contribute to the transition towards a circular economy."

[21] An exception in that context is the ban on the mixing of hazardous waste in Article 18 WFD.

[22] I.e. "(1) Cotton bud sticks, except if they fall within the scope of Council Directive 90/385/EEC or Council Directive 93/42/EEC; (2) Cutlery (forks, knives, spoons, chopsticks); (3) Plates; (4) Straws, except if they fall within the scope of Directive 90/385/EEC or Directive 93/42/EEC; (5) Beverage stirrers; (6) Sticks to be attached to and to support balloons, except balloons for industrial or other professional uses and applications that are not distributed to consumers, including the mechanisms of such sticks; (7) Food containers made of expanded polystyrene, i.e. receptacles such as boxes, with or without a cover, used to contain food which: (a) is intended for immediate consumption, either on-the-spot or take-away, (b) is typically consumed from the receptacle, and (c) is ready to be consumed without any further preparation, such as cooking, boiling or heating, including food containers used for fast food or other meal ready for immediate consumption, except beverage containers, plates and packets and wrappers containing food; (8) Beverage containers made of expanded polystyrene, including their caps and lids; (9) Cups for beverages made of expanded polystyrene, including their covers and lids."

4.4.3 Requirements

Requirements have become an increasingly applied instrument of Packaging Policy and Circular Economy. Against the backdrop of the concept of positive and negative conditionality,[23] requirements can also be understood as a positively formulated equivalent to the respectively corresponding negative ban in the antagonism of commandment and prohibition. This policy tool was applied in the former Article 9 PPWD for essential requirements of packaging as well as it is codified in Article 6 para. 1 SUPD, which stipulates, in order to prevent littering on the beaches of the EU according to Rec. 17 para. 1 sentence 1 SUPD, that single-use plastic products listed in part C[24] of the Annex that have caps and lids made of plastic may be placed on the market only, if the caps and lids remain attached to the containers during the product's intended use stage. Moreover, Articles 5 to 11 PPWR contain also detailed requirements for the sustainability of packaging.

4.4.4 Targets

Targets are a widespread tool of Packaging Policy and Circular Economy. Article 11 WFD contains a detailed targets regime for preparing for re-use and recycling to move, pursuant to Rec. 41 para. 1 sentence 1 WFD, towards a European recycling society with a high level of resource efficiency. In packaging law under the PPWD, the setting of targets has been used by the EU as measure for waste prevention of lightweight plastic carrier bags through the Member States,[25] for reusable packaging through the Member States,[26] and for recovery and recycling.[27] In the PPWR's scope of application, targets are a prescribed in the policy fields of minimum recycled content impact plastic packaging,[28] obligations related to refill,[29] re-use,[30] prevention of packaging waste,[31] deposit and return systems,[32] and recycling.[33] In the

[23] See for the notion of conditionality Schumacher (2012), pp. 142 sqq.; Jacobya and Hopkin (2020), pp. 1157 sqq.; Puente (2014), pp. 56 sqq.; Santiso (2003), pp. 1 sqq.

[24] I.e. "Beverage containers with a capacity of up to three litres, i.e. receptacles used to contain liquid, such as beverage bottles including their caps and lids and composite beverage packaging including their caps and lids, but not: (a) glass or metal beverage containers that have caps and lids made from plastic, (b) beverage containers intended and used for food for special medical purposes as defined in point (g) of Article 2 of Regulation (EU) No 609/2013 of the European Parliament and of the Council that is in liquid form."

[25] Article 4 para. 1a PPWD.

[26] Article 5 para. 1 sentence 2 lit. b PPWD.

[27] Article 6 para. 1 PPWD.

[28] Article 7 paras. 1, 2 PPWR.

[29] Article 28 para. 5 PPWR.

[30] Articles 29, 30 PPWR.

[31] Article 43 PPWR.

[32] Article 50 para. 5 PPWR.

[33] Articles 52 to 54 PPWR.

scope of single-use plastic law, targets are stipulated by the EU as action for national consumption reduction through the Member States,[34] for the content of recycled plastic in beverage bottles,[35] and for the separate collection for recycling.[36]

4.4.5 Information

Information is a traditional policy tool to empower the so-called "responsible consumer".[37] General waste law imposes the burden of consumer information on producers as a part of EPR[38] and on the Member States as a part of the obligation to take measures to prevent waste generation by developing and supporting information campaigns to raise awareness about waste prevention and littering.[39] Packaging law[40] demands, in addition to the general obligation to provide information as a part of EPR-regimes,[41] consumer information on and via the labelling of packaging[42] as well as about the prevention and management of packaging waste with regard to the role of end users in contributing to waste prevention, including any best practices,[43] re-use arrangements available for packaging,[44] the role of end users in contributing to the separate collection of packaging waste, materials, including handling of packaging containing hazardous products or waste,[45] the meaning of the labels and symbols affixed, printed or engraved on packaging in accordance with Article 12 PPWR or present in the documents accompanying the packaged product,[46] the impact of inappropriate discarding of packaging waste, for example as litter or in mixed

[34] Article 4 para. 1 subpara. 3 SUPD.

[35] Article 6 para. 5 SUPD.

[36] Article 9 para. 1 SUPD.

[37] See Lanzini (2017), pp. 15 sqq.; Lubowiecki-Vikuk et al. (2021), pp. 91 sqq.; Giesler and Veresiu (2014), pp. 840 sqq.; Dauses (1998), pp. 750 sqq.; Leisner (1991), pp. 498 sqq.; Kosek et al. (2020), pp. 214 sq.

[38] Article 8 para. 1 subpara. 2 sentence 2, Article 8a para. 2 sentence 1 para. 3 lit. e WFD.

[39] Article 9 para. 1 sentence 1, 2 lit. m WFD.

[40] The PPWD demanded consumer information about recovery and recycling targets through an information campaign for the general public and economic operators from the Member States (Article 6 para. 7 PPWD), about the composting properties of biodegradable and compostable plastic carrier bags from the European Commission (Article 6 para. 7 PPWD), and about the return, collection, and recovery systems available to the consumers, their role in contributing to reuse, recovery and recycling of packaging and packaging waste, the meaning of markings on packaging existing on the market, and the appropriate elements of the management plans for packaging and packaging waste as referred to in Article 14 PPWD by the Member States, also through the promotion of consumer information and awareness campaigns (Article 13 PPWD).

[41] Article 8a para. 2 sentence 1 WFD.

[42] Article 12 PPWR.

[43] Article 55 para. 1 subpara. 1 lit. a PPWR.

[44] Article 55 para. 1 subpara. 1 lit. b PPWR.

[45] Article 55 para. 1 subpara. 1 lit. c PPWR.

[46] Article 55 para. 1 subpara. 1 lit. d PPWR.

municipal waste, on the environment and on human health or the safety of persons and the adverse environmental impact of single-use packaging, in particular plastic carrier bags,[47] and the composting properties and appropriate waste management options for compostable packaging in accordance with Article 9 para. 2 PPWR, including that consumers shall be informed that compostable packaging is not suitable for home composting and that compostable packaging is not to be discarded in nature.[48] According to single-use plastic law, consumer information must further be provided by a conspicuous, clearly legible, and indelible marking on its packaging or on the product itself about appropriate waste management options for the product or waste disposal means to be avoided for that product, in line with the waste hierarchy, and the presence of plastics in the product and the resulting negative impact of littering or other inappropriate means of waste disposal of the product on the environment,[49] by publicly available information exchange and best practices concerning separate collection for recycling,[50] and by awareness raising measures about the availability of re-usable alternatives, re-use systems, and waste management options for those single-use plastic products and for fishing gear containing plastic as well as best practices in sound waste management carried out in accordance with Article 13 WFD, the impact of littering and other inappropriate waste disposal of those single-use plastic products and of fishing gear containing plastic on the environment, in particular on the marine environment, and the impact of inappropriate means of waste disposal of those single-use plastic products on the sewer network.[51]

4.4.6 Extended Producer Responsibility

European Packaging Policy and Circular Economy are deeply interwoven with Extended Producer Responsibility (EPR), which raises several questions about this concept, especially about its terminology, limitations, and implementation.

4.4.6.1 Terminology

EPR has been described as an environmental policy principle conceived for the incorporation of total product life cycle costs into production and consumption decisions.[52] According to Article 3 pt. 21 WFD, EPR schemes are legally defined as a set of measures taken by Member States to ensure that producers of products bear financial responsibility or financial and organizational responsibility for the management of the waste stage of a product's life cycle. This secondary law term must be interpreted and scrutinized in the light of the primary law polluter pays principle of Article 191 para. 2 subpara. 1 sentence 2 TFEU. Hence, EPR can, at least

[47] Article 55 para. 1 subpara. 1 lit. e PPWR.

[48] Article 55 para. 1 subpara. 1 lit. f PPWR.

[49] Article 7 para. 1 SUPD.

[50] Article 9 para. 2 sentence 2 SUPD.

[51] Article 10 SUPD.

[52] Compagnoni (2022), p. 1.

partially, be qualified as derivate of the polluter pays principle.[53] In reverse the legal EPR scheme definition of Article 3 pt. 21 WFD indicates that, pursuant to primary law interpretation of the legislative organs of the EU, the polluter pays principle of Article 191 para. 2 subpara. 1 sentence 2 TFEU does not only bear a purely financial responsibility,[54] but also possible organizational obligations,[55] which must consequently be compliant to the rights enshrined in the CFR and weight against each other under the terms of the principle of proportionality. This indication can additionally be supported from a historical perspective, since the polluter pays principle, which was first introduced in 1972 by the OECD against the backdrop of the principle of sustainable development[56] and functions, echoing, among other international conventions,[57] principle 16 Rio Declaration on Environment and Development,[58] as an instrument to internalize external costs,[59] can be perceived as a guiding maxim for the later development of the EPR concept originating from a report of *Thomas Lindhqvist* to the Swedish Ministry of Environment in 1990.[60] Ultimately, the literal formulation as principle "that the polluter should pay" does not oppose the interpretation of Article 191 para. 2 subpara. 1 sentence 2 TFEU as a legal basis for financial and organizational obligations, because other language versions provide a more open terminology, such as for example the legal term of the EU official German language version "*Verursacherprinzip*".

4.4.6.2 Limitations

Limitations of EPR may arise from its scope according to secondary law or the requirements of primary law. Since EPR provisions regularly contain only very few limitations, primary law, namely the polluter pays principle of Article 191 para. 2 subpara. 1 sentence 2 TFEU, gains practical relevance. These legal boundaries are particularly important, because EPR predominantly relies rather on a regulatory approach with mandatory obligations than a voluntary business strategy based on economic incentives aligned with environmental benefits.[61] The lack of clarity in the roles and responsibilities of stakeholders, especially importers, collectors and

[53] See also Kosior and Crescenzi (2020), p. 438; Dalhammer (2023), pp. 208 sqq.

[54] See Nettesheim (44th Update May 2011), Art. 191 AEUV para. 107.

[55] See Kahl (2018), Art. 191 AEUV paras. 97 sq.

[56] See Proelss (2023), pp. 45 sqq. recs. 27 sqq.

[57] See Wibisana (2006), p. 27.

[58] UN General Assembly (1992), Report of the UN Conference on Environment and Development, Rio de Janeiro, 3–14 June 1992, G.A. Report A/CONF.151/26, Vol. I, Resolutions adopted by the Conference (UN publication, Sales No. E.93.I.8 and corrigendum), Resolution 1, Annex I Principle 16: "National authorities should endeavour to promote the internalization of environmental costs and the use of economic instruments, taking into account the approach that the polluter should, in principle, bear the cost of pollution, with due regard to the public interest and without distorting international trade and investment." See also Weiss and Scherzer (2015), pp. 49 sqq.

[59] Calliess (2022b), Art. 191 AEUV para. 42; Kahl (2018), Art. 191 AEUV para. 97; Heine et al. (2020), pp. 99 sq.; O'Connor (1997), pp. 450 sqq.

[60] Gaur et al. (2022), pp. 375 sq.

[61] See Clift et al. (2022) pp. 46 sq.

recyclers, municipalities, consumers, and the producer responsibility organizations, are typically a major challenge in that context to ensure the effectiveness of EPR schemes.[62] Although the polluter pays principle sets limitations to EPR schemes and thus contourizes the outlines of the EPR notion, a systematic and specific CJEU case law, assuring legal certainty, has yet not been fully developed. The CJEU only has decided that the polluter pays principle requires natural causality between a pollution and the behavior of a polluter in the sense of a *conditio sine qua non.*[63] However, the causal link requirement is already fulfilled, if the competent authority has plausible evidence capable of justifying its presumption,[64] and the Member States have broad discretion when implementing an EPR scheme.[65] Beyond this, a further limitation of the polluter pays principle through the additional requirement of a normative causality appears to be a mandatory corrective in order to prevent inadequate results.[66] The distinction between the polluter pays principle and the burden sharing principle, respectively the fair and just distribution of burden, may function as a guiding directive in the precise demarcation of this normative causal link,[67] which also has been referred to under the term "relative share of responsibility".[68] The efficiency criterion, which demands an allocation of benefits of a certain pollution, can function as distinctive aspect in that context.[69] Socially adequate actions shall therefore not be qualified as normative causal behavoir under the scope of the polluter pays principle.[70]

---

[62] See Gaur et al. (2022), p. 376.

[63] ECJ, Judgment of 16 July 2009 – Case C-293/97 – The Queen v Minister of Agriculture, Fisheries, ex parte Standley et al., recs. 51 sqq.; Judgment of 24 June 2008 – Case C-188/07 – Commune de Mesquer, para. 82; Kahl (2018), Art. 191 AEUV para. 96; Lindhout and van den Broek (2014), pp. 48 sqq.

[64] ECJ, Judgement of 9 March 2010 – Case C-378/08 – ERG et al., para. 57.

[65] See ECJ, Judgement of 16 July 2009 – Case C-254/08 – Futura Immobiliare et al., recs. 48, 52, 55; Judgement of 9 March 2010 – Case C-378/08 – ERG et al., para. 55; Judgement of 4 March 2015 – Case C-534/13 – Fipa Group et al., paras. 46, 59.

[66] See also Nettesheim (44th Update May 2011), Art. 191 AEUV para. 110; Kahl (2018), Art. 191 AEUV para. 98.

[67] See also Nettesheim (44th Update May 2011), Art. 191 AEUV para. 109; Calliess (2022b), Art. 191 AEUV para. 42; Kahl (2018), Art. 191 AEUV para. 95.

[68] Heine et al. (2020), pp. 104 sq., 109 sq.

[69] See also ECJ, Judgement of 9 March 2010 – Case C-378/08 – ERG et al., para. 57; Nettesheim (44th Update May 2011), Art. 191 AEUV para. 109; Calliess (2022b), Art. 191 AEUV para. 41; Kahl (2018), Art. 191 AEUV para. 95.

[70] See also Kahl (2018), Art. 191 AEUV para. 82.

4.4.6.3 Implementation

The EU has successively implemented[71] EPR[72] in different policy areas, notably for the waste streams of packaging,[73] textiles,[74] batteries, electrical and electronic equipment, end-of life vehicles, paper, and oils.[75] Moreover, EPR has also been implemented for the quaternary treatment of micropollutants in urban wastewater.[76] With the adoption of Directive (EU) 2018/851, not only a legal definition of the term "extended producer responsibility scheme"[77] was added, but also the general provision on EPR was amended[78] and an additional provision on general minimum requirements for EPR schemes was inserted.[79] These amendments aimed to clarify a set of measues, either calling on the financial or financial and organizational responsibility of producers,[80] and to improve the governance and transparency of EPR schemes, while also reducing costs and the possibility of conflicts of interest emerging between organizations implementing EPR obligations on behalf of producers of products and waste operators that those organizations contract, and boosting performance.[81] In packaging law, EPR schemes are referred to as an incentive among other preventive measures[82] and an obligation for return, collection, and recovery systems.[83] Single-use plastic law generally prescribes the applicability of general waste law's EPR scheme definition of Article 3 pt. 21 WFD,[84] but also contains a special provision on EPR[85] considering that the relevance of some

---

[71] See for different instruments to implement the polluter pays principle Wibisana (2006), pp. 28 sqq.

[72] See for the conzeptualization of different EPR schemes Wong et al. (2016), pp. 60 sqq.; Gupta (2023), pp. 259 sqq.; Steenmans and Ulfbeck (2023), pp. 1 sq.; Nash and Bosso (2013), pp. 175 sqq.

[73] See for different international policies of plastic use and consumption Sin and Tueen (2023), pp. 255 sqq.; Förstner and Köster (2018), p. 559; Kosior and Crescenzi (2020), p. 438.

[74] Art. 22a WFD. See also European Commission (2022), EU Strategy for Sustainable and Circular Textiles, Communication of 30.3.2022, COM(2022) 141 final, p. 7; European Commission (2023), Circular economy for textiles: taking responsibility to reduce, reuse and recycle textile waste and boosting markets for used textiles, press release of 5.7.2023.

[75] Flanderka (2014), § 23 KrWG para. 2; Förstner and Köster (2018), p. 559; Kosior and Crescenzi (2020), p. 438; Alt (2018), pp. 177 sqq.

[76] Art. 9 sq. UWWTD. See also European Commission (2022), Proposal for a Directive of the European Parliament and of the Council concerning urban wastewater treatment (recast) of 26.10.2022, COM(2022) 541 final. See further also Schönfelder et al. (2025), pp. 189 sqq.; Homann and Franßen (2024), pp. 10 sqq.

[77] Article 3 pt. 21 WFD.

[78] Article 8 WFD.

[79] Article 8a WFD.

[80] Rec. 14 sentence 1 Directive (EU) 2018/851.

[81] Rec. 22 sentence 1 Directive (EU) 2018/851.

[82] Article 4 para. 1 subpara. 2 PPWD.

[83] Article 7 para. 2 PPWD.

[84] Article 3 pt. 10 SUPD.

[85] Article 8 SUPD.

requirements depends on the characteristics of the product.[86] This single-use plastics EPR encompasses for certain products the costs of awareness raising measures, waste collection for those products that are discarded in public collection systems, cleaning up litter resulting from those products and the subsequent transport and treatment of that litter, and data gathering and reporting.[87]

[86] Rec. 22 sentence 2 SUPD.

[87] Article 8 paras. 2 and 3 sentence 1 SUPD.

European Packaging Policy

5

Abstract

European Packaging Policy is embedded in a broader framework of strategic policy initiatives aimed at enabling a systemic sustainability transition. Core reference points include the Environment Action Programmes (EAP), the European Green Deal (EGD), the Clean Industrial Deal (CID), the New Circular Economy Action Plan (CEAP), and the European Strategy for Plastics. These policy frameworks articulate long-term visions, intermediate objectives, and sector-specific measures that redefine the role of packaging within sustainable production and consumption systems. The policy approach reflects a shift from isolated environmental measures towards an integrated transformation model that aligns environmental protection, economic competitiveness, innovation, and global responsibility. Packaging Policy thus emerges as a central element of the EU's overarching Circular Economy strategy.

While the preceding chapter has focused on the legal foundations of European packaging regulation, the broader policy context in which these rules are embedded must also be considered in order to understand their direction and coherence. The Packaging Policy[1] of the EU[2] is not the product of isolated legislative initiatives but is shaped by overarching strategic programmes that define long-term objectives, transformation pathways, and political priorities. The following chapter therefore examines the central policy conceptions that frame the development of packaging

[1] See also for Packaging Policy as component of Circular Economy on the different levels of international, european, national, municipal policies and strategies Wagner and Langer (2025a), pp. 223 sqq.; id. (2025b), pp. 307 sqq.

[2] See also for normative standardization through the ISO, CEN and DIN Wendenburg (2023), pp. 254 sqq.

R. H. D. Reimer, *Packaging Policy and Circular Economy*, Law for Professionals, https://doi.org/10.1007/978-3-032-27081-8_5

regulation within the wider agenda of sustainability, industrial transformation, and Circular Economy governance.

5.1 Environment Action Programmes

The EU's Environment Action Programmes[3] (EAP) deliver a guiding framework for Packaging Policy in a Circular Economy through a European Vision for 2050 and by means of a sustainability transition policy.

5.1.1 2050 Vision

With the 7th EAP for 2014 to 2020 the EU coins the vision, that in 2050, we live well, within the planet's ecological limits, that our prosperity and healthy environment stem from an innovative Circular Economy, where nothing is wasted and where natural resources are managed sustainably, and biodiversity is protected, valued and restored in ways that enhance our society's resilience, and that our low-carbon growth has long been decoupled from resource use, setting the pace for a safe and sustainable global society.[4] The EU's 8th EAP for 2022 to 2030 additionally declares as its long-term priority that by 2050 at the latest, people live well, within the planetary boundaries in a well-being economy where nothing is wasted, growth is regenerative, climate neutrality in the Union has been achieved and inequalities have been significantly reduced.[5] In line with this agenda[6] and building upon the European Green Deal,[7] the EU's 8th EAP functions as an environmental pillar for the implementation of its agenda 2030[8] and persues to accelerate the green transition to a climate-neutral, sustainable, resource-efficient, renewable energy-based, resilient, and competitive Circular Economy in a just, equitable, and inclu-

---

[3] See also in general on the EU's Environment Action Programmes in light of the UN Conference on the Human Environment in Stockholm in 1972 and behind the backdrop of the UN Environment Programme (UNEP) Kingston et al. (2017), pp. 82 sq.; Langlet and Mahmoudi (2016), pp. 28 sqq.; Migliore et al. (2020), pp. 1 sqq.; Halmaghi (2016), pp. 87 sqq.

[4] European Parliament and Council of the European Union (2013), Decision No 1386/2013/EU of the European Parliament and of the Council of 20 November 2013 on a General Union Action Programme to 2020 "Living well, within the limits of our planet", Annex para. 1.

[5] European Parliament and Council of the European Union (2022), Decision (EU) 2022/591 of the European Parliament and of the Council of 6 April 2022 on General Union Environment Action Programme to 2030, Article 2 para. 1 sentence 1.

[6] European Parliament and Council of the European Union (2022), Decision (EU) 2022/591 of the European Parliament and of the Council of 6 April 2022 on General Union Environment Action Programme to 2030, recs. 2, 3.

[7] European Parliament and Council of the European Union (2022), Decision (EU) 2022/591 of the European Parliament and of the Council of 6 April 2022 on General Union Environment Action Programme to 2030, Rec. 11.

[8] Council of the European Union (2019), The 8th Environment Action Programme—Turning the Trends Together, Council Conclusions of 4.10.2019, 12795/19, p. 6.

sive way to protect, restore, and improve the state of the environment by, inter alia, halting and reversing biodiversity loss.[9]

Among the 8th EAP's six interlinked thematic priority objectives, the EU aims to advance towards a well-being economy that gives back to the planet more than it takes and accelerates the transition to a non-toxic Circular Economy, where growth is regenerative, resources are used efficiently and sustainably, and the waste hierarchy is applied.[10] Environmental aspects of sustainability and significantly reducing key environmental and climate pressures related to the Union's production and consumption, in particular in the areas of energy, industry, buildings and infrastructure, mobility, tourism, international trade, and the food system shall be promoted.[11] According to this conzeptualization the EU relies on a tripartite priorization of protection, conservation, and enhancement of the EU's natural capital in order to turn the EU, amongst other prioritized objectives,[12] into a resource-efficient, green, and competitive low-carbon economy, whilst simultaneously safeguarding European citizens from environmemt-related pressures and risks to health or well-being.[13]

To turn the EU into a resource-efficient, green, and competitive low-carbon economy and in particular to promote Circular Economy, the EU uses a balanced mix of incentives for consumers and businesses, market-based instruments, and regulations to reduce the environmental impacts of their operations and products,[14] which encompasses clear and coherent labelling[15] and that Packaging shall be optimised to minimise environmental impacts.[16] In the field of waste management,

[9] European Parliament and Council of the European Union (2022), Decision (EU) 2022/591 of the European Parliament and of the Council of 6 April 2022 on General Union Environment Action Programme to 2030, Article 1 para. 2, Rec. 16.

[10] European Parliament and Council of the European Union (2022), Decision (EU) 2022/591 of the European Parliament and of the Council of 6 April 2022 on General Union Environment Action Programme to 2030, Article 2 para. 2 lit. c.

[11] European Parliament and Council of the European Union (2022), Decision (EU) 2022/591 of the European Parliament and of the Council of 6 April 2022 on General Union Environment Action Programme to 2030, Article 2 para. 2 lit. f.

[12] European Parliament and Council of the European Union (2013), Decision No 1386/2013/EU of the European Parliament and of the Council of 20 November 2013 on a General Union Action Programme to 2020 "Living well, within the limits of our planet", Article 2 para. 1 lit. c to l.

[13] European Parliament and Council of the European Union (2013), Decision No 1386/2013/EU of the European Parliament and of the Council of 20 November 2013 on a General Union Action Programme to 2020 "Living well, within the limits of our planet", Article 2 para. 1 lit. a, b, Annex para. 16 sentence 2 lit. a to c; Council of the European Union (2019), The 8th Environment Action Programme—Turning the Trends Together, Council Conclusions of 4.10.2019, 12795/19, p. 4.

[14] European Parliament and Council of the European Union (2013), Decision No 1386/2013/EU of the European Parliament and of the Council of 20 November 2013 on a General Union Action Programme to 2020 "Living well, within the limits of our planet", Annex para. 35 sentence 4.

[15] European Parliament and Council of the European Union (2013), Decision No 1386/2013/EU of the European Parliament and of the Council of 20 November 2013 on a General Union Action Programme to 2020 "Living well, within the limits of our planet", Annex para. 35 sentence 5.

[16] European Parliament and Council of the European Union (2013), Decision No 1386/2013/EU of the European Parliament and of the Council of 20 November 2013 on a General Union Action Programme to 2020 "Living well, within the limits of our planet", Annex para. 35 sentence 6.

including secondary raw materials markets,[17] and with the aim to move towards a lifecycle-driven Circular Economy with a cascading use of resources and residual waste that is close to zero,[18] the waste hierarchy's implementation is systematically based on market-based instruments and other measures that privilege prevention, recycling, and re-use, including EPR, while the development of non-toxic material cycles shall be supported.[19]

5.1.2 Sustainability Transition

The EAP's goals are set fourth through the political channels and tools to foster the EU's 2050 vision. In this context, the EU's Circular Economy Strategy 2.0 urges to integrate Circular Economy into all relevant policies and strategies and make it one of the cornerstones of the long-term vision of the EU's industrial future.[20] As part of the EU Plastics Strategy, Packaging Policy is considered as one of the key sectors for the EU's Circular Economy Strategies.[21] Overpackaging,[22] recyclability and sustainability of plastics and packaging,[23] microplastics,[24] toxcity of substances of

[17] European Parliament and Council of the European Union (2013), Decision No 1386/2013/EU of the European Parliament and of the Council of 20 November 2013 on a General Union Action Programme to 2020 "Living well, within the limits of our planet", Annex para. 40 sentence 4.

[18] European Parliament and Council of the European Union (2013), Decision No 1386/2013/EU of the European Parliament and of the Council of 20 November 2013 on a General Union Action Programme to 2020 "Living well, within the limits of our planet", Annex para. 40 sentence 6.

[19] European Parliament and Council of the European Union (2013), Decision No 1386/2013/EU of the European Parliament and of the Council of 20 November 2013 on a General Union Action Programme to 2020 "Living well, within the limits of our planet", Annex para. 35 sentence 5.

[20] Council of the European Union (2019), More circularity—Transition to a sustainable society, Council Conclusions of 4.10.2019, 12791/19, p. 8.

[21] Council of the European Union (2020), Draft Council conclusions on Making the Recovery Circular and Green of 11.12.2020, 13852/20, p. 16; Council of the European Union (2019), More circularity—Transition to a sustainable society, Council Conclusions of 4.10.2019, 12791/19, p. 12.

[22] Council of the European Union (2020), Draft Council conclusions on Making the Recovery Circular and Green of 11.12.2020, 13852/20, pp. 9, 15; Council of the European Union (2019), More circularity—Transition to a sustainable society, Council Conclusions of 4.10.2019, 12791/19, p. 12.

[23] Council of the European Union (2020), Draft Council conclusions on Making the Recovery Circular and Green of 11.12.2020, 13852/20, p. 15; Council of the European Union (2020), Draft Council conclusions on Making the Recovery Circular and Green of 11.12.2020, 13852/20, p. 9; Council of the European Union (2019), More circularity—Transition to a sustainable society, Council Conclusions of 4.10.2019, 12791/19, p. 12.

[24] Council of the European Union (2020), Draft Council conclusions on Making the Recovery Circular and Green of 11.12.2020, 13852/20, p. 17; Council of the European Union (2018), Delivering on the EU Action Plan for the Circular Economy, Council Conclusions of 25.6.2019, 10447/18, p. 9.

concern,[25] single-use plastics and products,[26] unsustainable production and consumption patterns,[27] and Policy Coherence for Sustainable Development (PCSD)[28] are intended to be specifically tackled as central policy fields. To ensure its sustainability transition, the EU relies on various tools and meachnisms, especially the implementation and application of secondary raw materials markets,[29] EPR (including EPR fee modulation),[30] digitalization, innovation, and new technologies (including satellite data, remote sensing, artificial intelligence, and eco-innovation),[31] an

[25] Council of the European Union (2020), Draft Council conclusions on Making the Recovery Circular and Green of 11.12.2020, 13852/20, pp. 9, 13; Council of the European Union (2019), More circularity—Transition to a sustainable society, Council Conclusions of 4.10.2019, 12791/19, p. 15; Council of the European Union (2019), Towards an ever more sustainable Union by 2030, Council Conclusions of 9.4.2019, 8286/19, p. 5; Council of the European Union (2018), Delivering on the EU Action Plan for the Circular Economy, Council Conclusions of 25.6.2019, 10447/18, pp. 7, 11 sqq.; Council of the European Union (2018), Eco-innovation: enabling the transition towards a circular economy, Council Conclusions of 18.12.2017, 15811/17, pp. 4, 7, 9.

[26] Council of the European Union (2020), Draft Council conclusions on Making the Recovery Circular and Green of 11.12.2020, 13852/20, p. 16; Council of the European Union (2019), More circularity—Transition to a sustainable society, Council Conclusions of 4.10.2019, 12791/19, p. 13.

[27] Council of the European Union (2019), More circularity—Transition to a sustainable society, Council Conclusions of 4.10.2019, 12791/19, p. 13.

[28] Council of the European Union (2019), Towards an ever more sustainable Union by 2030, Council Conclusions of 9.4.2019, 8286/19, p. 5.

[29] Council of the European Union (2020), Draft Council conclusions on Making the Recovery Circular and Green of 11.12.2020, 13852/20, pp. 7, 23 sq.; Council of the European Union (2019), The 8th Environment Action Programme—Turning the Trends Together, Council Conclusions of 4.10.2019, 12795/19, p. 8; Council of the European Union (2019), More circularity—Transition to a sustainable society, Council Conclusions of 4.10.2019, 12791/19, pp. 9, 16; Council of the European Union (2018), Delivering on the EU Action Plan for the Circular Economy, Council Conclusions of 25.6.2019, 10447/18, p. 7; Council of the European Union (2019), An EU Industrial Policy Stratetgy: a Vision for 2030, Council Conclusions of 27.5.2019, 9706/19, p. 11; Council of the European Union (2018), Eco-innovation: enabling the transition towards a circular economy, Council Conclusions of 18.12.2017, 15811/17, p. 9.

[30] Council of the European Union (2020), Draft Council conclusions on Making the Recovery Circular and Green of 11.12.2020, 13852/20, pp. 16, 22; Council of the European Union (2019), More circularity—Transition to a sustainable society, Council Conclusions of 4.10.2019, 12791/19, pp. 14, 16; Council of the European Union (2018), Delivering on the EU Action Plan for the Circular Economy, Council Conclusions of 25.6.2019, 10447/18, p. 7; Council of the European Union (2018), Eco-innovation: enabling the transition towards a circular economy, Council Conclusions of 18.12.2017, 15811/17, p. 7.

[31] Council of the European Union (2020), Draft Council conclusions on Making the Recovery Circular and Green of 11.12.2020, 13852/20, p. 7; Council of the European Union (2019), The 8th Environment Action Programme—Turning the Trends Together, Council Conclusions of 4.10.2019, 12795/19, p. 9; Council of the European Union (2019), More circularity—Transition to a sustainable society, Council Conclusions of 4.10.2019, 12791/19, pp. 12, 16; Council of the European Union (2019), An EU Industrial Policy Stratetgy: a Vision for 2030, Council Conclusions of 27.5.2019, 9706/19, pp. 8 sqq.; Council of the European Union (2018), Eco-innovation: enabling the transition towards a circular economy, Council Conclusions of 18.12.2017, 15811/17, pp. 3, 9 sqq.

EU Product Environmental Footprint (PEF),[32] labelling,[33] effective EU-wide market surveillance,[34] Responsible Business Conduct (RBC) and Corporate Social Responsibility (CSR),[35] and ecodesign in a circular bioeconomy on a sustainable products policy framework (including rethink, refuse, re-use, reduce, repair, redesign, and recycle in smart materials cycles, bio-based and biodegradable plastics, and circular service/business models).[36]

[32] Council of the European Union (2020), Draft Council conclusions on Making the Recovery Circular and Green of 11.12.2020, 13852/20, p. 10, Council of the European Union (2019), More circularity—Transition to a sustainable society, Council Conclusions of 4.10.2019, 12791/19, p. 15; Council of the European Union (2018), Eco-innovation: enabling the transition towards a circular economy, Council Conclusions of 18.12.2017, 15811/17, pp. 6, 10.

[33] Council of the European Union (2020), Draft Council conclusions on Making the Recovery Circular and Green of 11.12.2020, 13852/20, p. 15; Council of the European Union (2019), More circularity—Transition to a sustainable society, Council Conclusions of 4.10.2019, 12791/19, p. 15; Council of the European Union (2018), Delivering on the EU Action Plan for the Circular Economy, Council Conclusions of 25.6.2019, 10447/18, p. 8; Council of the European Union (2018), Eco-innovation: enabling the transition towards a circular economy, Council Conclusions of 18.12.2017, 15811/17, pp. 6, 8.

[34] Council of the European Union (2020), Draft Council conclusions on Making the Recovery Circular and Green of 11.12.2020, 13852/20, p. 27.

[35] Council of the European Union (2019), Towards an ever more sustainable Union by 2030, Council Conclusions of 9.4.2019, 8286/19, p. 8.

[36] Council of the European Union (2020), Draft Council conclusions on Making the Recovery Circular and Green of 11.12.2020, 13852/20, pp. 7, 9 sqq., 17, 21 sqq.; Council of the European Union (2019), The 8th Environment Action Programme—Turning the Trends Together, Council Conclusions of 4.10.2019, 12795/19, p. 8; Council of the European Union (2019), More circularity—Transition to a sustainable society, Council Conclusions of 4.10.2019, 12791/19, pp. 12 sq., 15 sq.; Council of the European Union (2018), Delivering on the EU Action Plan for the Circular Economy, Council Conclusions of 25.6.2019, 10447/18, pp. 7 sq., 19; Council of the European Union (2018), Eco-innovation: enabling the transition towards a circular economy, Council Conclusions of 18.12.2017, 15811/17, pp. 4 sqq.

5.2 European Green Deal

Within the spectrum of European policy frameworks, the European Green[37] Deal[38] (EGD) occupies a particularly prominent position as the central strategic reference point for the Union's sustainability transformation.[39] It provides the political narrative, strategic orientation, and long-term vision within which sector-specific initiatives, including Packaging Policy, are embedded and further developed. Against this background, the following section explores the Green Deal as a guiding policy framework that shapes the direction, ambition, and coherence of regulatory developments in the field of packaging and resource management.

5.2.1 Transformation Policy

The European Commission's policy under its EGD can be conzeptualized as transformation policy. In order to tackle climate and environmental-related challenges, the EGD aims to implement the United Nation's 2030 Agenda with its Sustainable Development Goals[40] and to transform the EU into a fair and prosperous society, with a modern, resource-efficient and competitive economy, where there are no net emissions of greenhouse gases in 2050 and where economic growth is decoupled from resource use.[41] The transformation policy contains a transformation on two sides, namely the green and digital transition—the so-called "twin transitions"—of the EU industry.[42] The EGD does not only deliver guidelines on the European envi-

---

[37] See for the notion of an "EU Blue Deal" European Economic and Social Committeef (2023), Opinion on the proposal for a Directive of the European Parliament and of the Council concerning urban wastewater treatment of 22.2.2023, 2023/C 146/06, OJ C 146/35, 27.4.2023, p. 35, para. 1.11.: "The EESC also calls on the European institutions to start addressing water as a priority and develop an 'EU Blue Deal': a redical effort to anticipate needs, to preserve water resources and adequately manage related challenges through a comprehensive and coordinated roadmap, setting ambitious targets and actions linked to agreed milestones. The EESC will make concrete proposals towards an EU Blue Deal in the course of 2023."

[38] European Commission (2019), The European Green Deal, Communication of 11.12.2019, COM(2019) 640 final.

[39] Note also the analysis of Bungard (2023), pp. 243 sqq.

[40] European Commission (2019), The European Green Deal, Communication of 11.12.2019, COM(2019) 640 final, p. 3.

[41] European Commission (2019), The European Green Deal, Communication of 11.12.2019, COM(2019) 640 final, p. 2; see also European Commission (2020), Communication of 11.3.2020, A New Circular Economy Action Plan. For a cleaner and more competitive Europe, COM(2020) 98 final, pp. 2 sq.

[42] European Commission (2019), The European Green Deal, Communication of 11.12.2019, COM(2019) 640 final, p. 7; European Commission (2021), Updating the 2020 New Industrial Strategy: Building a stronger Single Market for Europe's recovery, Communication of 5.5.2021, COM(2021) 350 final, p. 16; European Commission (2020), A New Industrial Strategy for Europe, Communication of 10.3.2020, COM(2020) 102 final, p. 9; see also European Commission (2018), A European Strategy for Plastics in a Circular Economy, Communication of 16.1.2018, COM(2018) 28 final, p. 1 for the term "transition".

ronment and economy policy, but also particular milestones and deliverables to achieve the goal by setting out a roadmap with key policies and key actions.[43]

5.2.2 Circular Economy Transformation

The EGD roadmap for Circular Economy Transformation consists of a mobilizing industrial strategy for a clean and circular economy.[44] Its objective is to transform the industrial sector and all the value chains within 25 years from 2025 until 2050.[45] The approach aims to support and accelerate the EU's industry transition to a sustainable model of inclusive growth by using Circular Economy's potential for new activities and jobs.[46] To achieve the key policy of Circular Economy Transformation, the EGD names six key actions, that are the EU industrial strategy, the Circular Economy Action Plan, initiatives to stimulate lead markets for climate neutral and circular products in energy intensive industrial sectors, the proposal to support zero carbon steel-making processes by 2030, legislation on batteries in support of the Strategic Action Plan on Batteries and the Circular Economy, and proposals of legislative waste reforms.[47]

According to the EGD, the Circular Economy Action Plan must be renewed to a New Circular Economy Action Plan behind the backdrop of the EU's industrial strategy[48] and including a sustainable products policy.[49] This New Circular Economy Action Plan intensifies the EU's ambitions on circularity. A common methodology and principles shall function as a basis of a circular design,[50] which formerly needed to be synched with the EU's ecodesign concept of the ErPD and which henceforth

[43] European Commission (2019), The European Green Deal, Communication of 11.12.2019, COM(2019) 640 final, pp. 2 sqq.; European Commission (2019), Annex to the Communication on the European Green Deal, Communication of 11.12.2019, COM(2019) 640 final, Annex.

[44] European Commission (2019), The European Green Deal, Communication of 11.12.2019, COM(2019) 640 final, pp. 9 sqq.; European Commission (2019), Annex to the Communication on the European Green Deal, Communication of 11.12.2019, COM(2019) 640 final, Annex.

[45] European Commission (2019), The European Green Deal, Communication of 11.12.2019, COM(2019) 640 final, p. 9.

[46] European Commission (2019), The European Green Deal, Communication of 11.12.2019, COM(2019) 640 final, p. 9.

[47] European Commission (2019), The European Green Deal, Communication of 11.12.2019, COM(2019) 640 final, pp. 9 sqq.; Annex to the Communication on the European Green Deal, Communication of 11.12.2019, COM(2019) 640 final, Annex.

[48] European Commission (2021), Updating the 2020 New Industrial Strategy: Building a stronger Single Market for Europe's recovery, Communication of 5.5.2021, COM(2021) 350 final; European Commission (2020), A New Industrial Strategy for Europe, Communication of 10.3.2020, COM(2020) 102 final; European Commission (2018), A European Strategy for Plastics in a Circular Economy, Communication of 16.1.2018, COM(2018) 28 final.

[49] European Commission (2019), The European Green Deal, Communication of 11.12.2019, COM(2019) 640 final, p. 7.

[50] European Commission (2019), The European Green Deal, Communication of 11.12.2019, COM(2019) 640 final, p. 7.

needs to be compliant with european ecodesign provisions of the the ESPR. The declared prioritization of reducing and reusing materials before recycling them and the setting out of minimum requirements to prevent environmentally harmful products from being placed on the EU market,[51] must be intertwined with the waste hierarchy of Article 4 WFD. The—in particular areas of European waste policy manifastating[52]—objective of strengthening EPR[53] correlates with the requirements of Article 8 sq. WFD and the polluter pays principle of Article 191 para. 2 subpara. 1 sentence 2 TFEU. A special focus is layed on plastics as a resource-intensive sector and their relevance as packaging, since the European Commission intends to ensure that all packaging in the EU market is reusable or recyclable in a economically viable manner by 2030, wants to develop a regulatory framework for biodegradable and bio-based plastics, and declares to implement measures on single-use plastics.[54]

Within the sustainable products policy, the EGD seeks to mobilze waste reduction potentials. That concerns notably targets and measures concerning over-packaging and waste generation, secondary raw materials and by-products, a Circular Plastics Alliance across value chains, an EU model for separate waste collection, and the export of waste outside of the EU.[55]

5.3 Clean Industrial Deal

The EU's Clean Industrial Deal[56] (CID) articulates a comprehensive policy vision that positions industrial competitiveness and deep decarbonisation not as competing objectives, but as mutually reinforcing pillars for the Union's long-term economic and geopolitical resilience. The CID explicitly frames industrial transformation as a matter of strategic security in a world marked by mounting geopolitical tensions, supply chain fragilities, and intensifying global competition for technological leadership. Within this ambitious framework, access to critical materials and the optimisation of material flows through circularity emerge as central determinants of the

[51] European Commission (2019), The European Green Deal, Communication of 11.12.2019, COM(2019) 640 final, p. 7.

[52] See for example Packaging Policy (Article 3 para. 2c, Article 4 para. 1 subpara. 2, Article 7 para. 2 PPWD), Plastics Policy (Article 8 SUPD), or Wastewater Policy (Article 9 sq. European Commission (2022), Proposal for a Directive of the European Parliament and of the Council concerning urban wastewater treatment (recast) of 26.10.2022, COM/2022/541 final).

[53] European Commission (2019), The European Green Deal, Communication of 11.12.2019, COM(2019) 640 final, p. 7.

[54] European Commission (2019), The European Green Deal, Communication of 11.12.2019, COM(2019) 640 final, pp. 7 sq.

[55] European Commission (2019), The European Green Deal, Communication of 11.12.2019, COM(2019) 640 final, p. 8.

[56] European Commission (2025), The Clean Industrail Deal: A roadmap for competitiveness and decarbonization, Communication of 26.2.2025, COM(2025) 85 final. See further also Huhta et al. (2025), pp. 95 sqq.

EU's ability to sustain advanced manufacturing, clean technologies, and energy-intensive sectors in a carbon-constrained future.[57]

5.3.1 Resource Security Policy

Notably, the CID does not consider resource efficiency as an ancillary objective, but embeds the strategic management of raw and secondary raw materials at the very heart of its industrial policy to empower Circular Economy by the implementation of the Critical Raw Materials Act. This reflects a profound recognition that the EU's existing resource dependencies, especially for materials essential to the energy transition and digital infrastructure, constitute structural vulnerabilities with implications for economic autonomy, jobs, and the fulfilment of climate objectives.[58]

The CID articulates a starkly pragmatic analysis of the EU's resource landscape mirroring the aim to foster sustainable and resilient production by the means of circularity. Critical raw materials are indispensable for sectors ranging from battery production to renewable energy technologies, yet the Union remains highly dependent on third-country suppliers for many of these inputs. The dependence on critical raw materials creates strategic vulnerabilities that are incompatible with the EU's aspirations for technological leadership, industrial autonomy, and climate neutrality.[59] To address this, the CID builds on and accelerates existing instruments—most notably the Critical Raw Materials Act—to embed resource security into the core of industrial policy.[60]

The EU's approach to resource security is multidimensional and fundamentally strategic. It aims first to mitigate supply risks by diversifying external sourcing and strengthening internal capacities for extraction, processing, and recycling of critical raw materials.[61] The establishment of mechanisms that enable European companies to aggregate demand and jointly procure critical materials represents a deliberate shift toward collective bargaining power in global markets. Such a mechanism, together with the creation of an EU-level Critical Raw Material Centre, is designed to generate economies of scale and improve negotiating leverage, which are essential when dealing with concentrated global supply chains dominated by a few major producers.[62]

---

57 European Commission (2025), The Clean Industrail Deal: A roadmap for competitiveness and decarbonization, Communication of 26.2.2025, COM(2025) 85 final, pp. 1 sq.

58 European Commission (2025), The Clean Industrail Deal: A roadmap for competitiveness and decarbonization, Communication of 26.2.2025, COM(2025) 85 final, pp. 14.

59 European Commission (2025), The Clean Industrail Deal: A roadmap for competitiveness and decarbonization, Communication of 26.2.2025, COM(2025) 85 final, pp. 1 sq.

60 European Commission (2025), The Clean Industrail Deal: A roadmap for competitiveness and decarbonization, Communication of 26.2.2025, COM(2025) 85 final, pp. 14.

61 European Commission (2025), The Clean Industrail Deal: A roadmap for competitiveness and decarbonization, Communication of 26.2.2025, COM(2025) 85 final, pp. 16 sqq.

62 European Commission (2025), The Clean Industrail Deal: A roadmap for competitiveness and decarbonization, Communication of 26.2.2025, COM(2025) 85 final, pp. 14.

Resource security is not confined to securing access to virgin inputs. The CID emphasises the strategic elevation of secondary raw materials as integral to supply resilience. This recognition stems from both economic and ecological imperatives. Economically, a robust secondary materials sector reduces the EU's exposure to volatile global markets and geopolitical disruptions. Ecologically, it advances material efficiency, curbs waste, and lowers the lifecycle emissions of industrial products. By sequencing resource security with circular strategies, the EU aims not merely to replace imported materials but to reconfigure value chains toward a more self-sustaining, resource-efficient industrial ecosystem to create a foundation for stable, predictable industrial growth that is resilient to external shocks and aligned with long-term decarbonisation pathways.[63]

5.3.2 Circularity Harmonization

Besides its Resource Security Policy, the CID equally foregrounds the need to reconcile linear production models with a systemic approach to circularity, not merely as waste management, but as market structuring and normative harmonisation across Member States via the so-called Circular Economy Act. In doing so, it lays the conceptual groundwork for harmonised legislative action that aligns the internal market with circular principles, enhances the supply of high-quality recycled materials, and strengthens resilience against external shocks.[64]

While raw material security addresses the supply side of industrial inputs, the CID also emphasises the role of circularity in rebalancing material flows and embedding sustainability into the structure of the internal market. Against this backdrop, the harmonization of the EU's Circular Economoy follows an approach of circularity that provides incremental improvements in recycling rates. Moreover, the CID envisages a systemic transformation of how materials are used, reused, recycled and circulated across the Union. This systemic perspective is a response to a landscape in which disparate national regulations, uneven recycling infrastructure, and fragmented markets for secondary raw materials have hindered the realisation of a fully cross-border Circular Economy in Europe.[65]

At the center of the strategic effort to intensify the harmonization of Circular Economy in the EU stands the European Circular Economy Act, which is conceived to accelerate the circular transition by enabling the free movement of circular products on the single market, secondary raw materials and waste, fostering a higher supply of high quality recyclates and stimulating demand for secondary materials and circular products while bringing down feedstock costs. It is intended to create a

[63] European Commission (2025), The Clean Industrail Deal: A roadmap for competitiveness and decarbonization, Communication of 26.2.2025, COM(2025) 85 final, pp. 1 sq., 14.

[64] European Commission (2025), The Clean Industrail Deal: A roadmap for competitiveness and decarbonization, Communication of 26.2.2025, COM(2025) 85 final, pp. 14 sqq.

[65] European Commission (2025), The Clean Industrail Deal: A roadmap for competitiveness and decarbonization, Communication of 26.2.2025, COM(2025) 85 final, pp. 14 sq.

genuine internal market for recycled and reusable materials by standardising criteria and dissolving regulatory barriers that currently inhibit the free movement of such materials between Member States. The harmonization of "end of waste" criteria, the reconceptualization of EPR via simplifying, digitalising and expanding the instrument in a targeted manner, and the stimulation of public procurement through respective criteria, serve as political tools to enact the Circular Economy Act. Through these measures, the Circular Economy Act aims to stabilize the supply and demand dynamics for secondary raw materials and to embed circularity into the very architecture of the EU's industrial markets.[66]

Nevertheless, the Circular Economy Act's ambition exceeds from a mere normative revision of the existing legal framework by proactively extending its effect—through incentives beyond bare regulatory harmonization—to stimulate market uptake of recycled content and circular products. By aligning procurement practices, quality standards, and investment incentives with circular principles, the Circular Economy Act seeks to shift industry behaviour and consumer demand in favour of circular solutions. Such alignment is intended to correct market distortions that have historically favoured primary over secondary materials, despite the latter's potential for reducing environmental impact and enhancing supply stability. Moreover, by integrating circularity into public procurement norms, the EU aims to leverage its considerable market power to accelerate the scaling of circular industries and to signal a stable, long-term policy trajectory that can catalyze private investment, especially through so-called Trans-Regional Circularity Hubs.[67]

5.4 New Circular Economy Action Plan

The EU's New Circular Economy Action Plan (CEAP)[68] describes Packaging Policy and Circular Economy in succession of the CEAP,[69] while containing a policy of "cleaner, more competitive, and co-creative" ("Tripple C Policy") after the EU's policy adjustment in order to react to the outcomes of the CEAP implementation report.

[66] European Commission (2025), The Clean Industrail Deal: A roadmap for competitiveness and decarbonization, Communication of 26.2.2025, COM(2025) 85 final, pp. 14 sq.

[67] European Commission (2025), The Clean Industrail Deal: A roadmap for competitiveness and decarbonization, Communication of 26.2.2025, COM(2025) 85 final, pp. 15 sq.

[68] European Commission (2020), A New Circular Economy Action Plan. For a cleaner and more competitive Europe, Communication of 11.3.2020, COM(2020) 98 final.

[69] European Commission (2015), Closing the loop—An EU action plan for the Circular Economy, Communication of 2.12.2015, COM(2015) 614 final.

5.4.1 Circular Economy Action Plan

In December 2015, the European Commission adopted its CEAP. This first systemtic Circular Economy Policy approach on an EU level and across entire value chains[70] addressed particularly SGD 12 of the UN 2030 Agenda and the G7 Alliance on Resource Efficiency[71] and contained actions in the fields of production, consumption, waste management, the market for secondary raw materials, sectorial actions (plastics, food waste, critical raw materials, construction and demolition, and biomass and bio-based materials), innovation and investment, and monitoring.[72] Waste management was considered as the vehicle for the waste hierarchy[73] effectuation[74] and it was concentrated on increased recycling targets for packaging materials,[75] high-quality recycling including the promotion of a voluntary certification of treatment facilities for certain key types of waste (e.g. plastics),[76] and improvements in waste collection and sorting, especially through EPR schemes and (other) economic instruments (e.g. landfill charges or pay-as-you-throw schemes[77]).[78] The CEAP turned to the potential of plastics on the market for secondary raw materials with regard to the absence of EU-wide standards, especially for high-grade recycling, secondary raw materials and recycled materials, and the need for clarification of end-of-waste rules in the distinction between waste and product.[79] Plastics were also identified as a priority area, which is essential for the transition to a

[70] European Commission (2019), Report on the implementation of the Circular Economy Action Plan, Report of 4.3.2019, COM(2019) 190 final, pp. 1 sq., 6 sqq.

[71] European Commission (2015), Closing the loop—An EU action plan for the Circular Economy, Communication of 2.12.2015, COM(2015) 614 final, p. 3.

[72] European Commission (2015), Annex to the Communication on Closing the loop—An EU action plan for the Circular Economy, Communication of 2.12.2015, COM(2015) 614 final, Annex 1.

[73] See Article 4 WFD.

[74] European Commission (2015), Closing the loop—An EU action plan for the Circular Economy, Communication of 2.12.2015, COM(2015) 614 final, p. 8.

[75] European Commission (2015), Closing the loop—An EU action plan for the Circular Economy, Communication of 2.12.2015, COM(2015) 614 final, pp. 8 sq.

[76] European Commission (2015), Closing the loop—An EU action plan for the Circular Economy, Communication of 2.12.2015, COM(2015) 614 final, pp. 8 sq.

[77] A pay-as-you-throw (PAYT) scheme is a policy concept, in which waste fees are paid according to the amount of mixed waste delivered to a waste management system and that is based in the EU on the polluter pays principle of Article 191 para. 2 TFEU; see also Elia et al. (2015), pp. 188 sqq.; Johnstone and Brown (2014), pp. 132 sqq.

[78] European Commission (2015), Closing the loop—An EU action plan for the Circular Economy, Communication of 2.12.2015, COM(2015) 614 final, pp. 9sq.

[79] European Commission (2015), Closing the loop—An EU action plan for the Circular Economy, Communication of 2.12.2015, COM(2015) 614 final, p. 11.

Circular Economy and that needs to be elaborted on in a strategy on plastics,[80] i.e. the later EU Plastics Strategy.[81]

5.4.2 Circular Economy Action Plan Implementation Report

In March 2019, the European Commission issued a report on the implementation of the CEAP.[82] According to this report, the ecodesign policy is considered as a possible opportunity for packaging, namely to improve packaging design for re-use and high-quality recycling of packaging.[83] The modernization of the waste management framework was reportedly achieved as goal through the entering into force of Directive (EU) 2018/852,[84] which revisied the PPWD.[85] In the matter of plastics, the European Commission reports the adoption of the EU Plastics Strategy[86] and lines out its function as a catalyzer for action that creates synergies between economic and environmental goals.[87] At the same time the European Commission identifies the necessity of more efforts to reach the objectives set out in the strategy and refers to the support of the Circular Plastics Alliance (CPA)[88] in the context of a multi-stakeholder engagement and collaboration along the value chain.[89] Tailored measures in the plastics sector[90] are according to the European Commission the ban of single-use plastics products and oxo-degradable plastics, the consumption reduction of plastic food containers and beverage bottles in conjunction with specific marking and labelling of certain products, percentage targets of recycled plastics in products (30% in beverage bottles as from 2030 and 25% in PET bottles as from 2025) and

[80] European Commission (2015), Closing the loop—An EU action plan for the Circular Economy, Communication of 2.12.2015, COM(2015) 614 final, pp. 13 sq.

[81] European Commission (2018), A European Strategy for Plastics in a Circular Economy, Communication of 16.1.2018, COM(2018) 28 final.

[82] European Commission (2019), Report on the implementation of the Circular Economy Action Plan, Report of 4.3.2019, COM(2019) 190 final.

[83] European Commission (2019), Report on the implementation of the Circular Economy Action Plan, Report of 4.3.2019, COM(2019) 190 final, p. 2.

[84] Directive (EU) 2018/852 of the European Parliament and of the Council of 30 May 2018 amending Directive 94/62/EC on packaging and packaging waste, OJ L 150, 14.6.2018, p. 141.

[85] European Commission (2019), Report on the implementation of the Circular Economy Action Plan, Report of 4.3.2019, COM(2019) 190 final, pp. 4 sq.

[86] European Commission (2018), A European Strategy for Plastics in a Circular Economy, Communication of 16.1.2018, COM(2018) 28 final.

[87] European Commission (2019), Report on the implementation of the Circular Economy Action Plan, Report of 4.3.2019, COM(2019) 190 final, pp. 6 sq.

[88] Circular Plastics Alliance (2019).

[89] European Commission (2019), Report on the implementation of the Circular Economy Action Plan, Report of 4.3.2019, COM(2019) 190 final, pp. 6 sq.

[90] See also the SUPD. See further European Commission (2020), A New Circular Economy Action Plan. For a cleaner and more competitive Europe, Communication of 11.3.2020, COM(2020) 98 final, p. 10.

of separate collection (90% of plastic bottles from 2029) in conjunction with design requirements (to connect caps to bottles), EPR schemes (covering the cost to clean-up litter), the reduction of plastic litter from ships, and the improvement of reporting obligations (for lost fishing gear, marking, and control of fishing gear for recreational fisheries).[91] The report concludes that not all possible areas are covered by the CEAP and that, even though the CEAP has accelerated the transition to a Circular Economy in an irreversible, global mega trend, more acceleration is needed to maintain the EU's Circular Economy leadership and ensure the fostering of Circular Economy as a competitive backbone of the EU industry.[92]

5.4.3 Triple C Policy

The European Circular Economy Policy under the New CEAP aims to provide a future-oriented agenda for achieving a cleaner and more competitive Europe in co-creation with economic actors, consumers, citizens, and civil society organisations on the behalf of an accelerated and EGD contributive Circular Economy transition towards a less primary materials dependent and sustainable economic system.[93] Therefore, the EU's Circular Economy Policy may also be paraphrased as "Triple C Policy"(cleaner, more competitive, and co-creative).

Under the Sustainable Product Policy framework, the New CEAP indetifies a lack of a comprehensive set of sustainability product requirements and of sufficient incentives to make products more circular, while simultaneously striving to reinforce waste prevention and recycling, especially during the product design phase.[94] In that context the New CEAP denominates the widening of the ecodesign framework, the establishment of sustainability principles (durability, reusability, upgradability, and reparaibility of products, increased recycling content in products, remanufacturing of high-quality recycling, carbon and environmental fooprints reduction, single-use restrictions and premature absolescene countering, a ban on the destruction of unsold durable goods,[95] products-as-a-service or other models of

---

[91] European Commission (2019), Report on the implementation of the Circular Economy Action Plan, Report of 4.3.2019, COM(2019) 190 final, p. 8.

[92] European Commission (2019), Report on the implementation of the Circular Economy Action Plan, Report of 4.3.2019, COM(2019) 190 final, pp. 10 sq.

[93] European Commission (2020), A New Circular Economy Action Plan. For a cleaner and more competitive Europe, Communication of 11.3.2020, COM(2020) 98 final, pp. 2 sq.; European Commission (2020), A New Industrial Strategy for Europe, Communication of 10.3.2020, COM(2020) 102 final, p. 9.

[94] European Commission (2020), A New Circular Economy Action Plan. For a cleaner and more competitive Europe, Communication of 11.3.2020, COM(2020) 98 final, pp. 3 sq.

[95] See also the German concept of "kreislaufwirtschaftsrechtliche Obhutspflicht" (duty of circular economical care) of § 23 para. 1 sentence 3, para. 2 no. 11, § 24 no. 10 KrWG. See further to this concept Petersen and Massow (2023), pp. 69 sqq.; Vogelsang (2023), pp. 5 sqq. and passim; Loschwitz (2023), pp. 75 sqq.; Beckmann (2023), pp. 113 sqq.; Reimer (2023), pp. 31 sqq.; Petersen (2022), pp. 927 sqq.; Petersen and Friedrich (2021) p. 5.

(E)PR, digitalization, rewards for sustainable performance, the improvement of coherence (of existing product regulating instruments along various phases of the product life circle), and effective and efficient enforcement (European Dataspace for Smart Circular Applications and concerted inspections/market surveillance actions) as opportune measures.[96]

In terms of the European Packaging Policy, the New CEAP gives notice of a further revision[97] of the PPWD with focus on the reduction of (over)packaging and packaging waste, driving design for re-use and recyclability of packaging and the reduction of the complexity of packaging materials.[98] European Packaging Policy and European Plastics Policy overlap through the New CEAP's announcement of mandatory requirements for recycled content and waste reduction measures for packaging as a key product, of microplastic reduction measures (restrictions, labelling, standardization, certification, regulation, and measuring), and of policy frameworks for bio-based, biodegradable, and compostable plastics.[99]

In its conclusion, the New CEAP stresses ultimately out that the Circular Economy transition will require the alignment and cooperation of all stakeholders at all levels[100] and be systematic, deep, and transformative, while also fair.[101]

5.5 European Strategy for Plastics

Among the policy initiatives that have significantly influenced the development of European Packaging Policy, the European Strategy for Plastics in a Circular Economy,[102] the so-called EU Plastics Strategy, represents a key conceptual build-

[96] European Commission (2020), A New Circular Economy Action Plan. For a cleaner and more competitive Europe, Communication of 11.3.2020, COM(2020) 98 final, pp. 4 sq.

[97] See European Commission (2022), Proposal for a Regulation of the European Parliament and of the Council on packaging and packaging waste, amending Regulation (EU) 2019/1020 and Directive (EU) 2019/904, and repealing Directive 94/62/EC of 30.11.2022, COM(2022) 677 final; European Commission (2022), Annexes 1 to 13 to the Proposal for a Regulation of the European Parliament and of the Council on packaging and packaging waste, amending Regulation (EU) 2019/1020 and Directive (EU) 2019/904, and repealing Directive 94/62/EC of 30.11.2022, COM(2022) 677 final, Annexes 1 to 13.

[98] European Commission (2020), A New Circular Economy Action Plan. For a cleaner and more competitive Europe, Communication of 11.3.2020, COM(2020) 98 final, pp. 8 sq.

[99] European Commission (2020), A New Circular Economy Action Plan. For a cleaner and more competitive Europe, Communication of 11.3.2020, COM(2020) 98 final, pp. 9 sq.

[100] European Commission (2020), A New Circular Economy Action Plan. For a cleaner and more competitive Europe, Communication of 11.3.2020, COM(2020) 98 final, p. 19.

[101] European Commission (2020), A New Circular Economy Action Plan. For a cleaner and more competitive Europe, Communication of 11.3.2020, COM(2020) 98 final, p. 19.

[102] European Commission (2018), A European Strategy for Plastics in a Circular Economy, Communication of 16.1.2018, COM(2018) 28 final; European Commission (2018), Annexes 1 to 3 to the Communication of a European Strategy for Plastics in a Circular Economy, Communication of 16.1.2018, COM(2018) 28 final, Annexes 1 to 3. See also European Commission (2018), Commission Staff Working Document accompanying the document A European Strategy for

ing block. It addresses plastics as a central material stream within the Circular Economy and formulates a targeted approach to restructuring production patterns, consumption practices, and end-of-life management. The following section therefore considers the strategic role of this policy initiative in shaping the transformation of the plastics sector and its broader implications for the evolution of packaging regulation in Europe.

5.5.1 Plastics Industry Reformation Policy

The cental objective of the EU Plastics Strategy is to rethink and improve the European plastics industry via establishing a strategic vision and by laying the foundations to a new (circular) plastics economy.[103] Hence, the EU Plastics Strategy's political concept may be adequately described as "Plastics Industry Reformation Policy". Considering the New Industrial Strategy, the EU Plastics Strategy could also be characterized as political approach to revolutionize the way we design, make, use, and get rid of things.[104] However, the EU Plastics Strategy is estimated as a catalyzer for action for the ambition of a Circular Economy transformation.[105] Furthermore, the CEAP report considers the EU Plastics Strategy also as an example of a Circular Economy Policy approach for many other sectors.[106] The Archimedean point of the EU Plastics Strategy as a strategic vision is the promotion of product reuse, repair, and recycling.[107] The particular components of this vision are broadly the same as the ones advocated in the CEAP and New CEAP.[108]

Plastics in a Circular Economy, Commission Staff Working Document of 16.1.2018, SWD(2018) 16 final.

[103] European Commission (2018), A European Strategy for Plastics in a Circular Economy, Communication of 16.1.2018, COM(2018) 28 final, pp. 1, 4 sqq.

[104] European Commission (2020), A New Industrial Strategy for Europe, Communication of 10.3.2020, COM(2020) 102 final, p. 9.

[105] European Commission (2019), Report on the implementation of the Circular Economy Action Plan, Report of 4.3.2019, COM(2019) 190 final, p. 6.

[106] European Commission (2019), Report on the implementation of the Circular Economy Action Plan, Report of 4.3.2019, COM(2019) 190 final, p. 10.

[107] European Commission (2018), A European Strategy for Plastics in a Circular Economy, Communication of 16.1.2018, COM(2018) 28 final, p. 5.

[108] See European Commission (2018), A European Strategy for Plastics in a Circular Economy, Communication of 16.1.2018, COM(2018) 28 final, p. 5; European Commission (2020), A New Circular Economy Action Plan. For a cleaner and more competitive Europe, Communication of 11.3.2020, COM(2020) 98 final, pp. 4 sqq.; European Commission (2015), Closing the loop—An EU action plan for the Circular Economy, Communication of 2.12.2015, COM(2015) 614 final, pp. 8 sqq.

5.5.2 Plastics Value Chain Transformation

The EU Plastics Strategy covers not only measures addressed to EU organs, but also contains key actions that are recommended for national and regional authorities and industry.[109] The European measures[110] take into account the improvement of the economics and quality of plastics recycling (design for recyclability, boost recycled content in products, and improve separate collection and sorting of plastic waste), the curbing of plastic waste and littering (single-use plastics reduction, tackle, monitor, and curb sea-based sources of marine litter, work on compostable and biodegradable plastics, and curbing microplastics pollution), the driving of investment and innovation towards a Cicular Economy, and the harnessing of global action.[111] Since the EU Plastics Strategy considers the various stages of a product in its way from "cradle to grave" or—in terms of a Circular Economy—"cradle to cradle", the EU's policy in this field might be accordingly described as policy of "Plastics Value Chain Transformation".[112] The multiple references to a revision of the PPWD and the introduction of EPR schemes demonstrate the key function of these prominent measures in the systematic approach of the EU Plastics Strategy.[113] Notably, the European Commission promotes frequently EPR schemes in the EU Plastics Strategy,[114] while at the same time the EU Plastics Strategy qualifies consumers and their awareness to make choices to avoid waste as key players to the Circular Economy transition.[115]

[109] European Commission (2018), A European Strategy for Plastics in a Circular Economy, Communication of 16.1.2018, COM(2018) 28 final, p. 6; European Commission (2018), Annexes 1 to 3 to the Communication of a European Strategy for Plastics in a Circular Economy, Communication of 16.1.2018, COM(2018) 28 final, Annexes 1 and 2.

[110] The recommended key actions for national and regional authorities and industry focus on the same principal guidelines. See European Commission (2018), Annexes 1 to 3 to the Communication of a European Strategy for Plastics in a Circular Economy, Communication of 16.1.2018, COM(2018) 28 final, Annex 2.

[111] European Commission (2018), A European Strategy for Plastics in a Circular Economy, Communication of 16.1.2018, COM(2018) 28 final, pp. 6 sqq; European Commission (2018), Annexes 1 to 3 to the Communication of a European Strategy for Plastics in a Circular Economy, Communication of 16.1.2018, COM(2018) 28 final, Annex 1.

[112] See also European Commission (2018), A European Strategy for Plastics in a Circular Economy, Communication of 16.1.2018, COM(2018) 28 final, p. 8: "Weak demand for recycled plastics is another obstacle to transforming the plastics value chain."

[113] European Commission (2018), A European Strategy for Plastics in a Circular Economy, Communication of 16.1.2018, COM(2018) 28 final, pp. 6 sqq; European Commission (2018), Annexes 1 to 3 to the Communication of a European Strategy for Plastics in a Circular Economy, Communication of 16.1.2018, COM(2018) 28 final, Annexes 1 and 2.

[114] European Commission (2018), A European Strategy for Plastics in a Circular Economy, Communication of 16.1.2018, COM(2018) 28 final, pp. 7 sq., 10, 11, 13, 15.

[115] European Commission (2018), A European Strategy for Plastics in a Circular Economy, Communication of 16.1.2018, COM(2018) 28 final, pp. 5 sq.

6 European Packaging Law Revision

Abstract

The revision of European Packaging Law constitutes a pivotal element of the EU's Circular Economy and sustainability agenda. It is characterized by a comprehensive regulatory approach that addresses the full life cycle of packaging and strengthens the binding nature of sustainability requirements. Key features include expanded material scope, enhanced recyclability and reusability obligations, minimum recycled content requirements, packaging minimization rules, and a reinforced system of Extended Producer Responsibility (EPR). The structural design and substantive content of the revised framework illustrate a transition from predominantly directive-based governance towards a more uniform and enforceable regulatory model. The revision therefore represents a qualitative shift in European Packaging Law, reflecting the EU's ambition to achieve a high level of environmental protection through systemic legal transformation.

By publishing the proposal for a Regulation on Packaging and Packaging Waste (PPWR) on 30th November 2022, the European Commission initiated a revision of European Packaging Law to substitute the PPWD, amend the MSR and the SUPD, and complement the ESPR in order to achieve climate neutrality under the European Climate Law. The proposal passed the European Parliament on 24th April 2024, was adopted by the Council of the European Union on 16th December 2024 and signed by the Presidents of the European Parliament and of the Council of European Union on 19th December 2024, before it was published in the EU's official journal on 22nd January 2025 and ultimately entered into force on 11th February 2025.[1] It shall apply from 12th August 2026[2] and is entirely applicable, also in regard to

[1] Article 71 para. 1 PPWR.

[2] Article 71 para. 2 PPWR.

R. H. D. Reimer, *Packaging Policy and Circular Economy*, Law for Professionals, https://doi.org/10.1007/978-3-032-27081-8_6

Article 67 para. 5 PPWR, from 12th February 2029.[3] This fundamental process in Packaging Policy and Circular Economy demands further elaboration on the context of the revision and the PPWR's structure and characteristics.

6.1 Context

The context of the revision of European Packaging Law may be subdivided and assessed by the aspects of the revision's objective, competence, and instrument, thereby providing a systematic framework for understanding both the rationale and the structural implications of the reform. This analytical differentiation makes it possible to capture the revision not merely as a technical legislative update, but as a fundamental transformation process within European Packaging Policy, in which regulatory intent, legal authority, and the chosen normative form interact to reshape the governance of packaging across its entire life cycle. At the same time, the triadic perspective highlights how political priorities, institutional competences, and regulatory techniques converge in the PPWR, allowing the revision to be interpreted as a deliberate step towards greater harmonisation, regulatory coherence, and a more effective implementation of Circular Economy objectives within the internal market.

6.1.1 Objective

According to the New CEAP the revision of the PPWD aims at a reduction of (over) packaging and packaging waste, driving design for re-use and recyclability of packaging and the reduction of the complexity of packaging materials.[4] Moreover, the EU's Policy under the New CEAP also encompasses mandatory requirements for recycled content and waste reduction measures for packaging as a key product, of microplastic reduction measures (restrictions, labelling, standardization, certification, regulation, and measuring), and of policy frameworks for bio-based, biodegradable, and compostable plastics.[5]

In order to implement this policy, the PPWR addresses issues and weaknesses of packaging law, which were identified through a fitness check in 2014, an evaluation study of 2020, and an impact assessment and extensive stakeholder consultation, and which were not addressed by the last amendment of the PPWD through Directive (EU) 2018/851.[6] Three main interlinked problems shall be tackled: grow-

[3] Article 71 para. 3 PPWR.

[4] European Commission (2020), A New Circular Economy Action Plan. For a cleaner and more competitive Europe, Communication of 11.3.2020, COM(2020) 98 final, pp. 8 sq.

[5] European Commission (2020), A New Circular Economy Action Plan. For a cleaner and more competitive Europe, Communication of 11.3.2020, COM(2020) 98 final, pp. 9 sq.

[6] European Commission (2022), Proposal for a Regulation of the European Parliament and of the Council on packaging and packaging waste, amending Regulation (EU) 2019/1020 and Directive (EU) 2019/904, and repealing Directive 94/62/EC of 30.11.2022, COM(2022) 677 final, pp. 2, 6.

ing packaging waste generation, barriers to packaging recycling and re-use, and low recycling quality in plastic packaging and use of secondary raw materials.[7] The PPWR's general objective is to reduce the negative impacts of packaging and packaging waste, while improving the functioning of the internal market, which is complemented by the specific objectives to reduce the generation of packaging of waste, promote a Circular Economy for packaging in a cost-efficient way, and promote the uptake of recycled content in packaging.[8]

6.1.2 Competence

According to the European Commission, it is appropriate to use the competence of Article 114 TFEU (internal market) as sole legal basis for the PPWR,[9] since traditional internal market legislation to create harmonized conditions for the placing on the market of packaging is concerned.[10] The European Commission justifies this evaluation by focusing on the function of packaging and on the indication, that barriers to the internal market do not only affect the free flow of packaging, but also of goods and services themselves.[11] EPR, particularly harmonized criteria for

---

[7] European Commission (2022), Proposal for a Regulation of the European Parliament and of the Council on packaging and packaging waste, amending Regulation (EU) 2019/1020 and Directive (EU) 2019/904, and repealing Directive 94/62/EC of 30.11.2022, COM(2022) 677 final, p. 8; European Commission (2022), Executive Summary of the Impact Assessment Report, Accompanying the document Proposal for a Regulation of the European Parliament and of the Council on packaging and packaging waste, amending Regulation (EU) 2019/1020 and Directive (EU) 2019/904, and repealing Directive 94/62/EC, Staff Working Document of 30.11.2022, SWD(2022) 385 final, p. 1.

[8] European Commission (2022), Impact Assessment Report, Accompanying the document Proposal for a Regulation of the European Parliament and of the Council on packaging and packaging waste, amending Regulation (EU) 2019/1020 and Directive (EU) 2019/904, and repealing Directive 94/62/EC, Staff Working Document of 30.11.2022, SWD(2022) 384 final, Part 1/2, pp. 5 sqq.; European Commission (2022), Executive Summary of the Impact Assessment Report, Accompanying the document Proposal for a Regulation of the European Parliament and of the Council on packaging and packaging waste, amending Regulation (EU) 2019/1020 and Directive (EU) 2019/904, and repealing Directive 94/62/EC, Staff Working Document of 30.11.2022, SWD(2022) 385 final, p. 1 sq. See also Kachur and Oehlmann (2023), pp. 20 sq.

[9] European Commission (2022), Impact Assessment Report, Accompanying the document Proposal for a Regulation of the European Parliament and of the Council on packaging and packaging waste, amending Regulation (EU) 2019/1020 and Directive (EU) 2019/904, and repealing Directive 94/62/EC, Staff Working Document of 30.11.2022, SWD(2022) 384 final, Part 2/2, Annex 5, p. 126. See also Kachur and Oehlmann (2023), p. 23.

[10] European Commission (2022), Proposal for a Regulation of the European Parliament and of the Council on packaging and packaging waste, amending Regulation (EU) 2019/1020 and Directive (EU) 2019/904, and repealing Directive 94/62/EC of 30.11.2022, COM(2022) 677 final, pp. 3 sq.

[11] European Commission (2022), Impact Assessment Report, Accompanying the document Proposal for a Regulation of the European Parliament and of the Council on packaging and packaging waste, amending Regulation (EU) 2019/1020 and Directive (EU) 2019/904, and repealing Directive 94/62/EC, Staff Working Document of 30.11.2022, SWD(2022) 384 final, Part 2/2, Annex 5, p. 125.

eco-modulation of EPR fees and the scope of EPR-related reporting, is also qualified as an instrument, which is based on Article 114 TFEU.[12]

In contrast to this exclusively internal market-based policy interpretation, it is evident that Packaging Policy and Circular Economy are a cross-sectional matter of economical and environmental questions. That implication has also been touched by the European Commission itself, who stated that further regulatory divergence bears the risks to lead to suboptimal impacts on the single market and the environment[13] and that a common PPWR framework will have a major impact on the recyclability of packaging and on the availability of secondary raw materials.[14] Moreover, the PPWR itself also refers to waste prevention and the reduction of the adverse impacts of packaging and packaging waste on the environment and human health, on the basis of a high level of environmental protection, as one of its subject matters in Article 1 para. 2 PPWR and in Rec. 2 PPWR. Furthermore, the PPWR addresses the environment as a regulatory aspect several times and in various regards.[15] Consequently, it convinces to not only consider Article 114 TFEU as sole legal basis for the PPWR, but also Article 191 para. 1 TFEU (environment) for those regulatory parts and/or provisions of the PPWR, which can be predominantly qualified as environmental question and which are not just a minor annex to an internal-market based regulatory complex.[16] That concerns notably EPR-related provisions, since EPR is broadly predetermined by the principles of Article 191 para. 2 subpara. 1 sentence 2 TFEU, especially the polluter pays principle.[17]

---

[12] European Commission (2022), Proposal for a Regulation of the European Parliament and of the Council on packaging and packaging waste, amending Regulation (EU) 2019/1020 and Directive (EU) 2019/904, and repealing Directive 94/62/EC of 30.11.2022, COM(2022) 677 final, p. 4; European Commission (2022), Impact Assessment Report, Accompanying the document Proposal for a Regulation of the European Parliament and of the Council on packaging and packaging waste, amending Regulation (EU) 2019/1020 and Directive (EU) 2019/904, and repealing Directive 94/62/EC, Staff Working Document of 30.11.2022, SWD(2022) 384 final, Part 2/2, Annex 5, p. 125.

[13] European Commission (2022), Impact Assessment Report, Accompanying the document Proposal for a Regulation of the European Parliament and of the Council on packaging and packaging waste, amending Regulation (EU) 2019/1020 and Directive (EU) 2019/904, and repealing Directive 94/62/EC, Staff Working Document of 30.11.2022, SWD(2022) 384 final, Part 2/2, Annex 5, p. 125.

[14] European Commission (2022), Proposal for a Regulation of the European Parliament and of the Council on packaging and packaging waste, amending Regulation (EU) 2019/1020 and Directive (EU) 2019/904, and repealing Directive 94/62/EC of 30.11.2022, COM(2022) 677 final, p. 4.

[15] See Articles 1, 3, 5, 6, 7, 8, 14, 25, 29, 34, 43, 48, 51, 53, 55, 58, 60, 61, 63, 69 PPWR and Recs. 2, 4, 9, 15, 17, 18, 19, 20, 24, 27, 31, 33, 36, 39, 43, 45, 46, 47, 48, 49, 51, 52, 53, 54, 57, 85, 91, 96, 102, 112, 113, 119, 127, 137, 148, 156, 161, 169, 170,175, 180, 183, 184, 188 PPWR.

[16] See also Engelmann (2024b), p. 228.

[17] See also Kosior and Crescenzi (2020), p. 438; Dalhammer (2023), pp. 208 sqq.

6.1.3 Instrument

The European Commission has developed three options for the revision of European Packaging Law, which namely consist of measures to increase standardisation and to establish clearer essential requirements that tend to be pre-requisites for measures of other groups (option 1), mandatory targets for waste reduction, re-use for certain sectors and minimum recycled content in plastic packaging, requirements to ensure full recyclability by 2030, and harmonized product rules (option 2), and higher mandatory targets than option 2 and additional product requirements (option 3).[18] The PPWR is based on option 2 as overall preferred choice by the European Commission.[19]

To transpose this policy into a legal shape under Article 288 TFEU, the Packaging Law Revision utilizes the instrument of a regulation instead of another amending directive. The purpose of this regulatory choice is the fostering of an efficient internal market through a new comprehensive set of regulatory solutions in order to provide more legal certainty, reduce distortion of competition, and send clear signals to non-EU market actors intending to place products on the EU market.[20] This instrumental shift from a directive to a regulation is based on the reduced effectiveness of the rules under the PPWD, which have evolved from uneven national regulatory frameworks and which jeopardize the transition to a decoupled and sustainable circular packaging economy.[21] The European Commission estimates the instrumental choice of a regulation in that context as only option to ensure more detailed and harmonized rules on the organization of collection and recovery processes and related responsibilities, including the rules that should apply to economic

---

[18] European Commission (2022), Proposal for a Regulation of the European Parliament and of the Council on packaging and packaging waste, amending Regulation (EU) 2019/1020 and Directive (EU) 2019/904, and repealing Directive 94/62/EC of 30.11.2022, COM(2022) 677 final, pp. 8 sqq.; European Commission (2022), Executive Summary of the Impact Assessment Report, Accompanying the document Proposal for a Regulation of the European Parliament and of the Council on packaging and packaging waste, amending Regulation (EU) 2019/1020 and Directive (EU) 2019/904, and repealing Directive 94/62/EC, Staff Working Document of 30.11.2022, SWD(2022) 385 final, p. 2.

[19] European Commission (2022), Proposal for a Regulation of the European Parliament and of the Council on packaging and packaging waste, amending Regulation (EU) 2019/1020 and Directive (EU) 2019/904, and repealing Directive 94/62/EC of 30.11.2022, COM(2022) 677 final, p. 11; European Commission (2022), Executive Summary of the Impact Assessment Report, Accompanying the document Proposal for a Regulation of the European Parliament and of the Council on packaging and packaging waste, amending Regulation (EU) 2019/1020 and Directive (EU) 2019/904, and repealing Directive 94/62/EC, Staff Working Document of 30.11.2022, SWD(2022) 385 final, pp. 2 sq.

[20] European Commission (2022), Proposal for a Regulation of the European Parliament and of the Council on packaging and packaging waste, amending Regulation (EU) 2019/1020 and Directive (EU) 2019/904, and repealing Directive 94/62/EC of 30.11.2022, COM(2022) 677 final, pp. 4 sq.

[21] European Commission (2022), Proposal for a Regulation of the European Parliament and of the Council on packaging and packaging waste, amending Regulation (EU) 2019/1020 and Directive (EU) 2019/904, and repealing Directive 94/62/EC of 30.11.2022, COM(2022) 677 final, p. 5.

operators.[22] The instrumental shift from a directive to a regulation will reflexively also affect the Member State's legal frameworks for packaging and packaging waste due to the necessity to adjust the national provisions to the standards set out in the PPWR.[23]

6.2 Structure

The PPWR contains a compehensive regime of Packaging Policy and Circular Economy.[24] It is accompanied by 13 annexes and subdivided into 188 recitals and 13 chapters consisting of 71 articles. The different chapters cover general provisions,[25] sustainability requirements,[26] labelling, marking and information requirements,[27] general obligations,[28] obligations of economoic operators to reduce packaging and packaging waste,[29] plastic carrier bags,[30] conformity of packaging,[31] management of packaging and of packaging waste,[32] safeguard procedures,[33] green public procurement,[34] delegated powers and committee procedure,[35] amendments,[36] and final provisions.[37] Chapter VIII on the management of packaging and packaging waste is further subdivided in seven sections containing general provisions,[38] waste prevention,[39] register of producers and EPR,[40] return, collection and deposit return

[22] European Commission (2022), Impact Assessment Report, Accompanying the document Proposal for a Regulation of the European Parliament and of the Council on packaging and packaging waste, amending Regulation (EU) 2019/1020 and Directive (EU) 2019/904, and repealing Directive 94/62/EC, Staff Working Document of 30.11.2022, SWD(2022) 384 final, Part 2/2, Annex 5, p. 127.

[23] See also Kachur and Oehlmann (2023), pp. 28 sqq.

[24] Note also the critical analysis of Engelmann (2024b), pp. 216 sqq.; id. (2024a), pp. 159 sqq.

[25] Chapter I PPWR.

[26] Chapter I PPWR.

[27] Chapter III PPWR.

[28] Chapter IV PPWR.

[29] Chapter V PPWR.

[30] Chapter VI PPWR.

[31] Chapter VII PPWR.

[32] Chapter VIII PPWR.

[33] Chapter IX PPWR.

[34] Chapter X PPWR.

[35] Chapter XI PPWR.

[36] Chapter XII PPWR.

[37] Chapter XIII PPWR.

[38] Chapter VIII Section 1 PPWR.

[39] Chapter VIII Section 2 PPWR.

[40] Chapter VIII Section 3 PPWR.

systems,[41] re-use and refill,[42] recycling targets and promotion of recycling,[43] and information and reporting.[44] The 13 annexes contain provisions about an indicative list of items in the scope of the definition of packaging waste in Article 3 para. 1 PPWR,[45] categories and parameters for assessment of recyclability of packaging,[46] compostable packaging,[47] the methodology for packaging minimization assessment,[48] restrictions on use of packaging formats,[49] requirements specific to the systems for re-use and refill stations,[50] the conformity assessment procedure,[51] the EU declaration of conformity,[52] information for registration and reporting to the register referred to in Article 44 PPWR,[53] minimum requirements for deposit and return systems,[54] the implementation plan to be submitted pursuant to Article 52 para. 2 pt. d PPWR,[55] data to be included by Member States in their databases on packaging and packaging waste,[56] and a correlation table.[57]

6.3 Characteristics

The PPWR contains four striking characteristics, which concern the PPWR's subject matter, packaging waste hierarchy, sustainability requirements, and extended packaging producer responsibility. Taken together, these elements reflect a shift towards a more comprehensive and life-cycle-oriented governance approach, in which environmental protection, market integration, and producer accountability are systematically interlinked. The following analysis therefore examines these characteristics not as isolated regulatory features, but as mutually reinforcing components of a coherent legal regime that aims to strengthen circularity, enhance legal certainty, and ensure the effective operationalization of sustainability requirements across the European packaging system.

[41] Chapter VIII Section 4 PPWR.

[42] Chapter VIII Section 5 PPWR.

[43] Chapter VIII Section 6 PPWR.

[44] Chapter VIII Section 7 PPWR.

[45] Annex I PPWR.

[46] Annex II PPWR.

[47] Annex III PPWR.

[48] Annex IV PPWR.

[49] Annex V PPWR.

[50] Annex VI PPWR.

[51] Annex VII PPWR.

[52] Annex VIII PPWR.

[53] Annex IX PPWR.

[54] Annex X PPWR.

[55] Annex XI PPWR.

[56] Annex XII PPWR.

[57] Annex XIII PPWR.

6.3.1 Subject Matter

Article 1 para. 1 PPWR contains a declaratory paraphrase of the regulation's policy agenda and describes therefore the regulation's subject matter in a narrower sense than the official title of Article 1 PPWR, which also encompasses the PPWR's contributions to the efficient functioning of the internal market in the sense of Article 1 para. 2 PPWR and the transition to a Circular Economy as well as to achieving climate neutrality at the latest by 2050 under Article 1 para. 3 PPWR. This new provision does not have an equivalent in the PPWD and is thus genuninely originating from the Packaging Law Revision.

6.3.1.1 Ratione Personae

With the regulatory shift from a directive to a regulation, legal obligations are generally no longer addressed exclusively to the Member States as layed down in Article 288 para. 3 TFEU, but directly applicable according to Article 288 para. 2 sentence 2 TFEU. This affects namely private entities, such as economic operators in the sense of Article 3 para. 1 subpara. 1 pt. 12 PPWR, who are in particular obligated under chapter V of the PPWR. Although the PPWR aims to empower consumers in the sense of Article 3 para. 1 subpara. 1 pt. 22 PPWR,[58] it does not explicitly grant the individual consumer any rights, but takes consumer interests into account in several provisions, especially in regard to consumer health,[59] consumer sorting through the laberling of packaging,[60] the refill of consumer containers in the take-away sector,[61] distance contracts with consumers via online-platforms under EPR,[62] the safety of consumers in re-use and refill systems,[63] and consumer information on prevention and management of packaging waste.[64]

6.3.1.2 Ratione Materiae

According to Article 1 para. 1 PPWR, the regulation concerns as well packaging as packaging waste. It contains requirements for packaging in terms of environmental sustainability and labelling, to allow its placing on the market, and stipulates requirements for packaging waste in matters of EPR, packaging waste prevention including the reduction of unnecessary packaging and the re-use or reduction of packaging, the collection of packaging waste and its treatment encompassing the recycling of packaging waste. The distinction between packaging and packaging waste correlates with a differentiated regime of legal consequences. While for

---

[58] European Commission (2022), Proposal for a Regulation of the European Parliament and of the Council on packaging and packaging waste, amending Regulation (EU) 2019/1020 and Directive (EU) 2019/904, and repealing Directive 94/62/EC of 30.11.2022, COM(2022) 677 final, p. 101.

[59] Article 11 para. 1 lit. c PPWR.

[60] Article 12 PPWR.

[61] Article 32 PPWR.

[62] Article 45 paras. 4, 7 PPWR.

[63] Article 51 PPWR.

[64] Article 55 PPWR.

packaging, the placing on the market is conceptualized as permissive requirement, the regulation follows an approach of reactive measures for packaging waste.

The details for placing packaging on the market are regulated in the free movement provision of Article 4 PPWR. According to Article 4 para. 1 PPWR, packaging shall only be placed on the market, if it complies with the PPWR. The peculiarities of the compliance assessment and relevance of conformity are further set out in Articles 35 to 39 PPWR. In case of formal non-compliance as listed in Article 62 para. 1 PPWR, the competent authority of a competent Member State shall, depending on the type of non-compliance, either take preventive measures pursuant to Article 62 para. 2 PPWR or restrictive measures, namely penalties, in line with Article 62 para. 3 and Article 68 PPWR. The preventive measures named in Article 62 para. 2 PPWR, i.e. all appropriate measures to prohibit the packaging being made available on the market or to ensure that it is recalled or withdrawn from the market, must be interpreted under the terms of Article 3 para. 1 subpara. 3 PPWR, which refers for typical market surveillance terms to the MSR.

The terms of EPR scheme, collection and treatment of packaging waste, re-use and refill of packaging are further defined through the reference of Article 3 para. 1 subpara. 2 PPWR to the WFD. However, any concretizing interpretation of these terms will also have to consider the specific preconditions and presumptions of the PPWR as *lex specialis*. Furthermore, the PPWR's terms must be seen in conjunction with the referral of Article 1 para. 3 PPWR to the waste hierarchy of Article 4 WFD.

6.3.1.3 Ratione Temporis

From a temporal perspective, Article 1 para. 1 PPWR is determined by the life cycle of packaging, which is legally defined in Article 3 para. 1 subpara. 1 pt. 67 PPWR as the consecutive and interlinked stages that packaging goes through, from raw material acquisition or generation from natural resources to final disposal.

The life cycle-term is furthermore determined in Rec. 17 PPWR on the basis of the packaging's design, which consequently renders the packaging's purpose the function of a criterion to interpret the legal definition. The reference to the packaging's design raises the question of the decisive perspective for the interpretation of the packaging's purpose. The fact that a private entity, for instance the designer of the packaging, could decide on the temporal applicability of the PPWR, if a subjective perspective was applied, is not in line with the regulatory approach of establishing a comprehensive regime with a clear scope as layed down in Article 2 PPWR and is thus barely convincing. An objective perspective from the point of view of a neutral third party with the necessary expertise seems in that context to be rather appropriate, since hereby the legal system and the ratio of the PPWR and other European law can be taken into account to interpret a packaging's puropose based on its design in a particular case.

Another concretizing description of the life cycle term contains Rec. 17 PPWR by denominating the period from manufacture to use and end-of life, including, waste management, as stages of the life cycle of packaging. Behind the backdrop of the Circular Economy approach, the cradle-to-cradle principle,[65] and the reference of Article 3 para. 1 subpara. 2 PPWR to the waste management term of Article 3 pt. 9 WFD, the definition of the end-of-waste status[66] and thus the demarcation between packaging waste and a new product, such as for example secondary raw materials at the end of a recycling process, become a determining aspect for the temporal applicability of the PPWR.

6.3.2 Packaging Waste Hierarchy

Article 1 para. 3 PPWR declares the waste hierarchy of Article 4 WFD applicable for packaging and packaging waste and aims pursuant to Rec. 15 PPWR in line with the life cycle thinking to deliver the best overall environmental outcome, especially with regard to the use of recycled content in packaging during the production and reducing the amount of packaging during the placing on the market in terms of its volume and weight. The provision of Article 1 para. 3 PPWR hereby differs from the packaging waste hierarchy of Article 1 para. 2 PPWD.[67] The packaging waste hierarchy correlates with additional provisions on waste prevention,[68] on re-use and refill,[69] and on recycling targets and promotion of recycling.[70] The recovery and disposal of packaging waste—the two lowest-ranked priorities of the waste hierarchy—are not regulated by the PPWR and remain thus governed by the *lex generalis* of the WFD. Political tools used to effectuate the packaging waste hierarchy are the setting of targets for the prevention and recycling of packaging waste and the prescription of requirements for re-use and refill systems according to Annex VI PPWR. Measures to implement the packaging waste hierarchy are according to Article 43 para. 5 PPWR trade-barrier-free and competitive-neutral incentives, especially economic instruments, and are limited by the principles of proportionality and non-discrimination, which is declaratory vis-à-vis the correlating primary law requirements.

6.3.3 Sustainability Requirements

Articles 5 to 11 PPWR formulate detailed specifications for the sustainability of packaging. These provisions include requirements for substances in packaging,[71]

---

[65] See for the cradle-to-cradle principle Becker (2018), pp. 31 sqq.; Zhang et al. (2023), pp. 2 sqq.; Kalmykova et al. (2018), pp. 194 sq.; Voorthuis and Gijbels (2010), pp. 372 sqq.

[66] See in that context also the general rule of Article 6 WFD.

[67] See Reimer (2022), pp. 165 sqq.

[68] Article 43 PPWR.

[69] Article 51 PPWR.

[70] Articles 52 to 54 PPWR.

[71] Article 5 PPWR.

recyclable packaging,[72] minimum recycled content in plastic packaging,[73] biobased feedstock in plastic packaging,[74] compostable packaging,[75] packaging minimization,[76] and reusable packaging.[77]

6.3.3.1 Requirements for Substances in Packaging

Article 5 PPWR aims to minimize the level of risk, which derives from the presence and concentration of substances of concern in packaging material or packaging components, and refers in order to ensure this objective to the early stage of manufacturing.[78] The provision further intends to ensure the balance with other sustainability requirements. Therefore, it takes into account that the extent of recyclability requirements can be limited by the impacts on chemical safety[79] as far as the concerned substances signify an acceptable risk to human health and environment.[80] The details of this approach are specified in delegated acts[81] by the European Commission as competent institution and under the assistance of the European Chemicals Agency.[82] In addition to the EU declaration of conformity,[83] the technical documentation of Annex VII PPWR renders further information on the compliance with the sustainability requirements.[84]

6.3.3.2 Recyclable Packaging

Article 6 PPWR implements a central objective of the European Commission's New CEAP[85] by generally declaring that all packaging shall be recyclable by 2030, acknowledging only a few exceptions according to Article 6 para. 11 PPWR. Furthermore, recyclability shall also function—on the basis of a recyclability performance grade and in consideration of technical feasibility and economic viability—as modulation criterion for the determination of the financial contributions that must be paid by producers to comply with their EPR obligations.[86]

---

[72] Article 6 PPWR.

[73] Article 7 PPWR.

[74] Article 8 PPWR.

[75] Article 9 PPWR.

[76] Article 10 PPWR.

[77] Article 11 PPWR.

[78] Article 5 para. 1 PPWR.

[79] See further for the entanglement of Circular Economy and chemicals legislation Kropp (2024), pp. 259 sqq.

[80] Article 290 TFEU.

[81] Article 5 para. 2 subpara. 2 PPWR.

[82] Article 5 paras. 7, 8 PPWR.

[83] Article 39, Annex VIII PPWR.

[84] Article 5 para. 6 PPWR.

[85] European Commission (2020), A New Circular Economy Action Plan. For a cleaner and more competitive Europe, Communication of 11.3.2020, COM(2020) 98 final, p. 8.

[86] Article 6 para. 8 PPWR.

The requirements to recyclability are defined in Article 6 para. 2 PPWR, namely through the packaging's design for material recycling[87] and the packaging's waste capacity of separate collection and waste stream sorting,[88] and by the specifications of the European Commission's delegated acts[89] under Article 6 para. 4 PPWR and its implementing acts[90] under Article 6 para. 5 PPWR. During a five-year period, innovative packaging may enter the market although it is non-compliant.[91]

The recyclability requirements are linked in multiple ways to the legal definitions of Article 3 PPWR and are therefore correspectively predetermined in their scope. Relevant legal definitions that must paticuliarly be taken into account, when assessing the recyclability of a packaging, are those of design for recycling,[92] recyclability,[93] packaging waste recycled at scale,[94] material recycling,[95] high-quality recycling,[96] innovative packaging,[97] secondary raw materials,[98] waste,[99] and separate collection.[100] Moreover, the term recyclability[101] must be interpreted in conjunction with the general legal definition of recycling,[102] which stipulates that recycling means any recovery operation by which waste materials are reprocessed into products, materials or substances whether for the original or other purposes, and which includes the reprocessing of organic material, but does not include energy recovery and the reprocessing into materials that are to be used as fuels or for backfilling operations.

6.3.3.3 Minimum Recycled Content in Plastic Packaging

Article 7 PPWR must be seen in conjunction with Articles 52 to 54 PPWR and prescribes percentual targets for a certain minimum of recycled content in plastic packaging. Immediate packaging,[103] contact sensitive plastic packaging of medical devices, devices exclusively destined for research use and certain investigational devices,[104] contact sensitive plastic packaging of certain in vitro diagnostics medical

[87] Article 6 para. 2 subpara. 1 lit. a PPWR.

[88] Article 6 para. 2 subpara. 1 lit. b PPWR.

[89] Article 290 TFEU.

[90] Article 291 TFEU.

[91] Article 6 para. 10 PPWR.

[92] Article 3 para. 1 subpara. 1 pt. 37 PPWR.

[93] Article 3 para. 1 subpara. 1 pt. 38 PPWR.

[94] Article 3 para. 1 subpara. 1 pt. 39 PPWR.

[95] Article 3 para. 1 subpara. 1 pt. 40 PPWR.

[96] Article 3 para. 1 subpara. 1 pt. 40 PPWR.

[97] Article 3 para. 1 subpara. 1 pt. 46 PPWR.

[98] Article 3 para. 1 subpara. 1 pt. 47 PPWR.

[99] Article 3 para. 1 subpara. 1 pt. 2 PPWR.

[100] Article 3 para. 1 subpara. 2 PPWR, Article 3 pt. 11 WFD.

[101] Article 3 para. 1 subpara. 1 pt. 38 PPWR.

[102] Article 3 para. 1 subpara. 2 PPWR, Article 3 pt. 17 WFD.

[103] Article 7 para. 4 lit a PPWR.

[104] Article 7 para. 4 lit b PPWR.

devices,[105] certain outer packaging in cases where such is necessary to comply with specific requirements to preserve the quality of the medical product,[106] compostable plastic packaging,[107] certain packaging used for the transport of dangerous goods,[108] contact sensitive plastic packaging for food that is intended only for infants and young children, food for special medical purposes and certain packaging for drinks and food typically used for young children,[109] and packaging of supplies, components and immediate packaging components for the manufacturing of certain medical products, where such packaging is needed to be in line with the quality and standards of the medical product,[110] plastic packaging that is intended to come into contact with food where the quantity of recycled content poses a threat to human health and results in non-compliance of packaged products with the FCMFR,[111] and any plastic part representing less than 5% of the total weight of the whole packaging unit[112] are excluded from the obligations under Article 7 PPWR. The percentage of recycled content used in packaging shall also be another criterion for the modulation of EPR obligations.[113]

6.3.3.4 Biobased Feedstock and Plastic Packaging

Regarding biobased plastic packaging the European Commission is prospectively entitled to review the state of technological development and environmental performance, while taking into consideration the sustainability criteria laid down in Article 29 RED II.[114] The term "biobased plastics" means plastics made from biological resources, such as biomass feedstock, organic waste or by-products, and irrespective of whether the plastics are biodegradable or non-biodegradable.[115] Based on the results of the review of the state of technological development and environmental performance, the European Commission is obligated to draft a legislative proposal in order to lay down sustainability requirements for biobased feedstock in plastic packaging,[116] targets to increase the use of biobased feedstock in plastic packaging,[117] introduce the possibility to achieve the targets for minimum recycled content in plastic packaging[118] by using biobased plastic feedstock instead of recycled content recovered from post-consumer plastic waste in the event that

[105] Article 7 para. 4 lit c PPWR.

[106] Article 7 para. 4 lit d PPWR.

[107] Article 7 para. 4 lit. e PPWR.

[108] Article 7 para. 4 lit. f PPWR.

[109] Article 7 para. 4 lit. g PPWR.

[110] Article 7 para. 4 lit. h PPWR.

[111] Article 7 para. 5 lit. a PPWR.

[112] Article 7 para. 5 lit. b PPWR.

[113] Article 7 para. 7 PPWR.

[114] Article 8 para. 1 PPWR.

[115] Article 3 para. 1 subpara. 1 pt. 53 PPWR.

[116] Article 8 para. 2 lit. a PPWR.

[117] Article 8 para. 2 lit. b PPWR.

[118] Article 7 paras. 1, 2 PPWR.

suitable recycling technologies for food-contact packaging complying with the requirements laid down in the RPFCMR are not available,[119] and amend, where appropriate, the definition of biobased plastic set out in Article 3 para. 1 subpara. 1 pt. 53 PPWR.[120]

6.3.3.5 Compostable Packaging

Compostable packaging is legally defined as packaging that biodegrades in industrially controlled conditions or that is capable of undergoing biological decomposition in such conditions, including through anaerobic digestion, but not necessarily in a home-composting environment, combined, if necessary, with physical treatment, resulting ultimately in the conversion of the packaging into carbon dioxide or, in the absence of oxygen, methane, and mineral salts, biomass and water, and that does not hinder or jeopardise the separate collection and the composting and anaerobic digestion process.[121] Against this backdrop, certain permeable beverage bags[122] and sticky labels attached to fruit and vegetables are mandatorily required to be compatible with the standard for composting in industrially controlled conditions in bio-waste treatment facilities, when they are placed on the market.[123] The Member States can additionally stipulate that the formentioned packaging must fulfill the standards for home-composting as far as they have been determined by the the European standardization organisations according to European Commission's mandate to request such further regulation.[124] Certain non-permeable beverage systems,[125] composed of other than metal, very lightweight plastic carrier bags,[126] and lightweight plastic carrier bags,[127] as well as packaging that already has been required to be compostable by national law in the past before the applicability of the PPWR may also be bound by national law to be compostable, if they are within the scope of a national bio-waste system[128] according to which waste with similar biodegradability and compostability properties as bio-waste can be collected together with bio-waste, which encompasses appropriate waste collection schemes, and which guarantees a waste treatment infrastructure that ensures compostable packaging to enter the bio-waste management stream.[129] Other packaging must be designed for material recycling without affecting the recyclability of other waste streams.[130]

---

[119] Article 8 para. 2 lit. c PPWR
[120] Article 8 para. 2 lit. d PPWR.
[121] Article 3 para. 1 subpara. 1 pt. 50 PPWR.
[122] Article 3 para. 1 subpara. 1 pt. 1 lit. f PPWR.
[123] Article 9 para. 1 PPWR.
[124] Article 9 paras. 1, 6 PPWR.
[125] Article 3 para. 1 subpara. 1 pt. 1 lit. g PPWR.
[126] Article 3 para. 1 subpara. 1 pt. 57 PPWR.
[127] Article 3 para. 1 subpara. 1 pt. 56 PPWR.
[128] Article 22 para. 1 WFD.
[129] Article 9 para. 2 PPWR.
[130] Article 9 para. 3 PPWR.

6.3.3.6 Packaging Minimization

Article 10 para. 1 PPWR must be seen in conjunction with the obligation related to excessive packaging[131] and concerns the eco-design of packaging in terms of a weight and volume reduction to the minimum necessary for ensuring the functionality of the packaging, while also considering the packaging's shape and material. Except for packaging, which is protected by certain design rights or associated with a geographical indication protected under European law, packaging is generally subject to a ban from the market, if it does not comply with the packaging minimization performance criteria specifications[132] or if it posseses characteristics that aim only to increase the perceived volume of the product, including double walls, false bottoms, and unnecessary layers.[133] The details of packaging minimization standards are subject to further regulation by the European standardization organizations on the basis of the European Commission's mandate to request such further regulation.[134]

6.3.3.7 Reusable Packaging

In the scope of the PPWR, the the term "re-use" is legally defined as any operation by which reusable packaging is used again multiple times for the same purpose for which it was conceived,[135] whereas the concept of "preparing for re-use" is determined by the general definition of Article 3 pt. 16 WFD.[136] Moreover, the expression "re-use system" means the organisational, technical or financial arrangements together with incentives, that allow re-use either in a closed loop or open loop system, such as a deposit and return system that ensures that packaging is collected for re-use.[137] Furthermore, the legal definitions related to re-use and the provision of Article 11 PPWR must be seen in conjunction with the obligations under Articles 26 to 33 and 51 PPWR. According to Article 11 para. 1 PPWR packaging can only be considered to be reusable, if it has been conceived, designed, and placed on the market with the objective to be re-used multiple times,[138] has been conceived and designed to accomplish as many rotations as possible under normally predictable conditions of use,[139] fulfills applicable requirements regarding consumer health, safety and hygiene,[140] can be emptied or unloaded without being damaged in a way that would prevent its further function and re-use,[141] is capable of being emptied, unloaded, refilled or reloaded while maintaining the quality and safety of the

---

[131] Article 24 PPWR.

[132] Annex IV PPWR.

[133] Article 10 para. 2 PPWR.

[134] Article 10 para. 3 PPWR.

[135] Article 3 para. 1 subpara. 1 pt. 27 PPWR.

[136] Article 3 para. 2 PPWR.

[137] Article 3 para. 1 subpara. 1 pt. 31 PPWR.

[138] Article 11 para. 1 lit. a PPWR.

[139] Article 11 para. 1 lit. b PPWR.

[140] Article 11 para. 1 lit. c PPWR.

[141] Article 11 para. 1 lit. d PPWR.

packaged product and ensuring compliance with the applicable safety and hygiene requirements, including those on food safety,[142] is capable of being reconditioned in accordance with the specific requirements to re-use systems concerning reconditioning,[143] while maintaining its ability to perform its intended function,[144] allows for affixing of labels and the provision of information on the properties of that product and on the packaging itself, including any relevant instructions and information for ensuring safety, adequate use, traceability and shelf-life of the product,[145] can be emptied, unloaded, refilled or reloaded without risk to the health and safety of those responsible for doing so,[146] and fulfills the requirements specific to recyclable packaging,[147] so that it can be recycled when it becomes waste.[148] The minimum number of rotations for reusable packaging[149] for the packaging formats which are most frequently used in re-use are further concretized through delegated acts[150] by the European Commission, which also take into account hygiene and other requirements such as logistics.[151]

6.3.4 Extended Packaging Producer Responsibility

The PPWR introduces packaging law standards for EPR and thus establishes basic rules for a European Extended Packaging Producer Responsibility, which raises questions about the regulatory instrument, the general content, and the structure of the administrative procedure, namely the registration and authorization proceedings.

6.3.4.1 Regulatory Instrument

As a regulation in the sense of Article 288 para. 2 TFEU, the PPWR's Extended Packaging Producer Responsibility directly addresses private entities, particularly producers and producer responsibility organizations. Consequently, the PPWR's EPR provisions[152] are directly applicable to producers and other obligated private entities, if the Member States are not in particular addressed as entities in charge. In contrast to the regulatory instrument of a directive, the PPWR's EPR obligations have—persuant to their content—a vertical direct effect between the EU and the

142 Article 11 para. 1 lit. e PPWR.
143 Annex VI part B PPWR.
144 Article 11 para. 1 lit. f PPWR.
145 Article 11 para. 1 lit. g PPWR.
146 Article 11 para. 1 lit. h PPWR.
147 Article 6 PPWR.
148 Article 11 para. 1 lit. i PPWR.
149 Article 11 para. 1 lit. b PPWR.
150 Article 290 TFEU.
151 Article 11 para. 2 PPWR.
152 Articles 44 to 47 PPWR.

private entity concerned, for instance the obligations to register[153] and to apply for authorization,[154] and a horizontal direct effect between private entities, for example the right of providers of online platforms to obtain certain information on the registration and to demand a self-certification of such producers directly from these producers.[155] However, the PPWR does not introduce a genuine European EPR scheme for packaging and packaging waste, as it refers to the general notion of extended producer responsibility schemes in the sense of Article 3 pt. 21 WFD.[156] The PPWR neither establishes a European register of producers in responsibility and under the competence of the European Commission nor a European producer responsibility organization. The institutional requirements of Articles 44 to 47 PPWR, in particular the transposition of the administrative procedure and hence the details of an organizational and structural conceptualization of an EPR scheme, are left to the Member States, who must—similar to an obligation from a directive—implement the PPWR's standards into national law.

6.3.4.2 General Content

The revision of European Packaging Law extends the regulatory density of EPR in the field of Packaging Policy and Circular Economy and introduces a European Extended Packaging Producer Responsibility. While the PPWD scarcely refers to EPR[157] and exclusively in the sense of Article 8 and 8a WFD, the provisions of Articles 44 to 47 PPWR provide a *lex specialis* with a more detailed framework on EPR for producers of packaging, which is systematically embedded in and interwoven with the *lex generalis* EPR regime of the WFD. The European Extended Packaging Producer Responsibility concerns the establishment and obligations regarding a register of producers,[158] EPR requirements,[159] the entrustment of a producer responsibility organization,[160] and the authorization of EPR fulfillment by the competent authority.[161] Even though the revision enhances, in addition to Article 8a para. 4 subpara. 1 lit. a WFD and in consideration of transparency, proportionality, non-discrimination, and efficiency,[162] the extent of EPR costs in the field of labelling waste recepticales for the colletion of packaging waste[163] and carrying out certain compositional surveys of collected mixed municipal waste,[164] the PPWR statutes encompass rather a regulatory amendment of EPR by a procedural approach than

[153] Article 44 para. 2 PPWR.

[154] Article 47 para. 1 PPWR.

[155] Article 45 para. 4 PPWR.

[156] Article 3 para. 1 subpara. 2 PPWD.

[157] Article 3 pt. 2c, Article 4 para. 1 subpara. 2, Article 7 para. 2 PPWD.

[158] Article 44 PPWR.

[159] Article 45 PPWR.

[160] Article 46 PPWR.

[161] Article 47 PPWR.

[162] Article 45 para. 2 subpara. 2 PPWR.

[163] Article 45 para. 2 subpara. 1 lit. a PPWR.

[164] Article 45 para. 2 subpara. 1 lit. b PPWR.

the stipulation of substantial requirements, which specifically address packaging and packaging waste. The subject matter of European Extended Packaging Producer Responsibility is predominantely determined by Article 45 PPWR, which refers, similar to Article 7 para. 2 PPWD, to Article 8 and 8a WFD. The administrative procedure, on the opposite, is broardly regulated under the European Extended Packaging Producer Responsibility concept enshrined in Articles 44 to 47 PPWR and can be thus basically characterized as a two-tiered proceeding of registration and authorization.

6.3.4.3 Registration Proceeding

The register of producers, which must be established by the Member States, serves to monitor compliance of the producer's EPR obligations.[165] Until the grant of a registration, the PPWR stipulates a self-executing prohibition to make packaging available on the market.[166] Hence, producers are incentivized to fulfill their obligation to apply for registration.[167] The application must be submitted via an electronic data-processing system, in each Member State where producers make packaging available for the first time and can be subject to cost-based and proportionate fees.[168] The requested information must generally encompass the aspects mentioned in Annex IX part A pt. 1 PPWR[169] and Annex IX part B pt. 1 PPWR[170] as far as the particular clauses to provide the information of Annex IX part B pt. 2 PPWR for *de-minimis*-cases of less than 10 tonnes during one calender year[171] or to provide the information of Annex IX part B pt. 3 PPWR in the case of the fulfillment of EPR through re-use systems[172] do not apply. If the applying producer has submitted all necessary information, the competent authority grants the registration and provides a registration number within a maximum period of 12 weeks.[173] In terms of transparency, the Member States are obligated to ensure that providers of online platforms are granted access, free of charge, to the information in the register, if they allow consumers to conclude distance contracts with producers,[174] which is supplemented by a right to claim certain information on the registration and to demand a self-certification of such producers directly from these producers.[175] Once the registration is completed, the producer is obligated to notify to the competent authority any changes to the submitted information and of any correlating permanent

---

[165] Article 44 para. 1 PPWR.
[166] Article 44 para. 4 PPWR.
[167] Article 44 para. 2 sentence 1 PPWR.
[168] Article 44 para. 2, para. 11 lit. a, d PPWR.
[169] Article 44 para. 4 PPWR.
[170] Article 44 para. 7 PPWR.
[171] Article 44 para. 8 PPWR.
[172] Article 44 para. 10 PPWR.
[173] Article 44 paras. 5, 6, 11 lit. b PPWR.
[174] Article 44 para. 13 PPWR.
[175] Article 45 para. 4 PPWR.

cessation of the making available on the market.[176] Moreover, the producer is obligated to periodically report on certain information to the competent authority after the registration each calender year by first June.[177] This information is partly also subject to the obligation of producer responsibility organizations to publish on their websites, at least every year, information on the quantity of packaging, including packaging of packaged products, made available for the first time on the territory of a Member State, or unpacked by a producer without being an end user, and on the levels of recovered and recycled materials in relation to the quantity of packaging for which they have been performing producer responsibility obligations.[178]

6.3.4.4 Authorization Proceeding

At the initial stage of the authorization proceeding, producers in the case of individual EPR fulfillment or entrusted producer responsibility organizations in case of collective EPR fulfillment are required to apply for an authorization on fulfillment of EPR from the competent authority.[179] If a Member State has not implemented collective EPR fulfillment as mandatory, producers are entitled to entrust an authorized producer responsibility organization at their own discretion.[180] Producer responsibility organizations (PRO) are legally defined as a legal entity that financially or financially and operationally organizes the fulfillment of EPR obligations on behalf of several producers.[181] PRO must be required by the national law to cover the whole territory of the respective Member State[182] and are subject to oversight by an independent third party or the competent authority for the EPR obligations with respect to their fulfillment in a coordinated manner.[183] The verification of an application for authorization must be done by a competent authority or an independent expert, who is obligated to issue a verification report.[184] After the verification, the obligation to authorize[185] is succeeded by an obligation to notify changes to the submitted information in the application and in terms of the authorization or the permanent cessation of operations[186] and the competent authority may amend the authorization.[187] In a case of non-compliance, the competent authority is entitled to revoke the authorization.[188] Ultimately, the obligation for authorization is supplemented by an obligation to provide an adequate guarantee, which may be a public

[176] Article 44 para. 12 sentence 1 PPWR.

[177] Article 39 para. 7 PPWR.

[178] Article 46 para. 4 subpara. 1 PPWR.

[179] Article 47 para. 1 PPWR.

[180] Article 46 para. 1 PPWR.

[181] Article 3 para. 1 subpara. 1 pt. 66 PPWR.

[182] Article 46 para. 2 sentence 1 PPWR.

[183] Article 46 para. 2 sentence 2 PPWR.

[184] Article 47 para. 2 sentence 5 PPWR.

[185] Article 46 para. 1 PPWR.

[186] Article 47 para. 4 sentence 1 PPWR.

[187] Article 47 para. 4 sentence 2 PPWR.

[188] Article 47 para. 5 PPWR.

fund that is financed by producers' fees and for which a Member State is jointly and severally liable and which must be intended to cover the costs related to EPR waste management operations in any case of non-compliance or insolvency.[189] In contrast to an unregistered market access,[190] the PPWR does not stipulate a self-executing prohibition to make packaging available on the market in case of unauthorized conduct, but obligates the Member States to establish measures that ensure compliance with the requirements for the authorization procedure.[191]

[189] Article 47 para. 6 PPWR.
[190] Article 44 para. 4 PPWR.
[191] Article 47 para. 3 PPWR.

Conclusion

7

Abstract

European Packaging Policy has become a central component of the EU's Circular Economy, reaching far beyond traditional waste management and influencing production structures, market organization, and patterns of consumption across the entire value chain. It is embedded not only in the EU's internal sustainability agenda, but also in the broader framework of international environmental governance, particularly under the auspices of the UN and its objectives on sustainable consumption, resource efficiency, and plastic pollution. The current legal framework reflects a comprehensive approach that seeks to align environmental protection, internal market coherence, and economic competitiveness within a consistent regulatory architecture, while positioning Packaging Policy as a strategic instrument of structural transformation. In doing so, European Packaging Policy operates at the intersection of sustainability objectives, industrial modernization, and multilateral engagement, reinforcing the EU's capacity to contribute to and influence emerging global standards. Its practical impact will depend on coherent implementation, institutional coordination, and the ability of economic actors and infrastructures to adjust to evolving regulatory expectations, thereby shaping the long-term effectiveness of the Circular Economy as a governance model.

This concluding section draws together the central findings of the analysis and places them within a broader interpretative perspective, thereby linking the individual strands of argument developed throughout the study into a coherent overall assessment. By synthesising the legal, institutional, and policy-related dimensions that shape European Packaging Policy, it becomes possible to identify the structural patterns that define the EU's approach to the Circular Economy and to evaluate the

R. H. D. Reimer, *Packaging Policy and Circular Economy*, Law for Professionals, https://doi.org/10.1007/978-3-032-27081-8_7

extent to which the current regulatory framework contributes to a long-term transformation towards sustainability. At the same time, the conclusion provides an opportunity to reflect on the dynamic nature of this policy field, highlighting both the progress achieved and the challenges that remain in ensuring regulatory consistency, effective implementation, and continued development in light of evolving environmental and economic demands.

7.1 Summary

This summary consolidates the essential results of the preceding analysis and brings them into a structured and condensed form. In this vein, the main results of the analysis may be summarized in the subsequent way by the following core theses:

1. The UN 2030 Agenda contains a new agenda of 17 Sustainable Development Goals (SDG) with 169 associtated targets and considers achieving such a sustainable urban development and management—among other measures—through a reduction and recycling of waste.
2. According to UN SDG 12, which demands to "[e]nsure sustainable consumption and production patterns[1]", the sustainable management and efficient use of natural resources, concretized in the environmentally sound management of all wastes throughout their life circle by 2020, are variables for the implementation of the UN 2030 Agenda.
3. The UN Environment Programme (UNEP) functions as secretariat for the Intergovernmental Negotiating Committee (INC) on Plastic Pollution, publishes contributions on Sustainable Consumption and Production (SCP) Policies to decouple economic growth from environmental degradation and is subject to multiple demands for an institutional reform to establish a respective International Organization, for instance as UN Environment Organization (UNEO), UN Environment Protection Organization (UNEPO) or World Environment Organization (WEO).
4. The UN Environment Assembly (UNEA) has delivered significant resolutions on plastics and microplastics in the context of marine litter and Circular Economy, especially regarding single-use plastic products pollution, innovative pathways to achieve sustainable consumption and production, and efforts towards an international legally binding instrument to end plastic pollution.
5. The UN Plastic Pollution Treaty is a—under the management of the INC—negotiated internationally legally binding instrument on plastic pollution, which is designated to addresses the full life cycle of plastic, taking into account, among other factors, the principles of the Rio Declaration on Environment and Development, as well as national circumstances and capabilities, and a catalogue of various further aspects.

[1] UN General Assembly (2015), Transforming our world: the 2030 Agenda for Sustainable Development, G.A. Res. A/RES/70/1 (21 October 2015), p. 22.

6. The European Commission's DG ENV Strategic Plan 2020–2024 (Environment) identifies Circular Economy as "Specific Objective 1: The EU economy is more circular and uses natural resources and products more sustainably" and measures its policy outcome by the Number of EU Ecolabel products,[2] eco-innovation index,[3] municipal waste generation and treatment,[4] export of waste outside the EU,[5] and proportion of proposed legislative revisions that include burden reduction measures.[6]
7. The European Commission's Directorate Green Dipolmacy & Multilateralism (DG ENV.F) aims to take over global leadership in order to externalize its Global Circular Economy Policy for the Global Alliance on Circular Economy and Resource Efficiency (GACERE), which includes measures to identify knowledge and governance gaps, take forward partnership initiatives, mobilise its neighbors and partners, build alliances with the like-minded, and apply policy dialogues.
8. The European External Action Service (EEAS) promotes—in the context of the "Green Deal Diplomacy"—its Climate, Environment & Energy Diplomacy in the EU's External Relations through bilateral cooperation to encourage the adoption of energy and resource-efficient, low carbon, and circular growth models suitable for the local conditions.
9. The European Environment Agency (EEA) and its European Environment Information and Observation Network (Eionet) are important think tanks for Packaging Policy and Circular Economy.
10. The European Parliament's Committee on the Environment, Public Health, and Food Safety (ENVI) has published notable (draft) reports for Packaging Policy and Circular Economy under the support of the European Parliamentary Research Service's (EPRS) Panel for the Future of Science and Technology (STOA),
11. European Packaging Legislation relies in general either on Article 114 TFEU (internal market) or on Article 191 para. 1 TFEU (environment) as legal basis.
12. European Packaging Policy and Circular Economy are determined by the precautionary principle, the prevention principle, the rectification at source principle, and the polluter pays principle of Article 191 para. 2 subpara. 1 sentence 2 TFEU and the environmental principles of integration and sustainability of Article 11 TFEU and Article 37 CFR, which inherently call for proportional balancing and equilibration with other principles and optimization against other conflicting interests.
13. The regulatory system of European Packaging Policy is shaped by a multi-layered interaction between general Circular Economy law and sector-specific packaging regulation. Packaging law operates within this system as a special-

[2] Result indicator 1.1.

[3] Result indicator 1.2.

[4] Result indicator 1.3.

[5] Result indicator 1.4.

[6] Result indicator 1.5.

ised legal field that both derives from and contributes to the broader Circular Economy framework. Its regulatory logic is characterised by policy alignment, legal convergence, and institutional interlinkages, with the Waste Framework Directive (WFD) functioning as the central normative reference point. This embedded structure ensures coherence across legal spheres while allowing for differentiated regulatory responses to the specific environmental, economic, and functional characteristics of packaging and packaging waste.

14. The waste hierarchy, bans, requirements, targets, information, and EPR are policy instruments to integrate and transfer the EU's Packaging Policy into secondary law.
15. European Packaging Policy is governed by the *lex generalis* waste hierarchy of Article 4 WFD and *lex specialis* waste hierarchy provisions for certain policy areas, such as the former Article 1 para. 2 PPWD in Packaging Policy. The packaging waste hierarchy of Article 1 para. 2 PPWD correlated formerly with the subsequent Articles 4 to 6 PPWD, which contain further requirements on prevention, reuse, recovery, and recycling, and is now addressed by Article 1 para. 3 PPWR.
16. Neither the WFD nor the PPWD rely largely on bans, while the SUPD is—at least partially—an example of a rather prohibitionist policy.
17. Requirements have become an increasingly applied instrument of Packaging Policy and Circular Economy and can also be understood as a positively formulated equivalent to the respectively corresponding negative ban in the antagonism of commandment and prohibition.
18. Targets are a widespread tool of Packaging Policy and Circular Economy, notably in the WFD, the PPWD, the PPWR, and the SUPD.
19. Information is a traditional policy tool to empower the so-called "responsible consumer".
20. European Packaging Policy and Circular Economy are deeply interwoven with Extended Producer Responsibility (EPR).
21. European secondary law EPR must be interpreted and scrutinized in the light of the primary law polluter pays principle of Article 191 para. 2 subpara. 1 sentence 2 TFEU and can thus, at least partially, be qualified as derivate of the polluter pays principle.
22. Although the polluter pays principle sets limitations to EPR schemes and thus contourizes the outlines of the EPR notion, a systematic and specific CJEU case law, assuring legal, certainty has yet not been fully developed.
23. The EU has successively implemented EPR in different policy areas, notably for the waste streams of packaging, batteries, electrical and electronic equipment, end-of life vehicles, paper, and oils, and is currently proposing EPR for the quaternary treatment of micropollutants in urban wastewater and for textiles.
24. The Packaging Policy of the EU is defined by the European Green Deal, the Clean Industrial Deal, the New Circular Economy Action Plan, and the European Strategy for Plastics.

25. The European Green Deal (EGD) conzeptualizes Packaging Policy and Circular Economy on the basis of a transformation policy and the Circular Economy transformation.
26. The EGD transformation policy is conzeptualiued as so-called "twin transitions" towards a green and digital transition and aims to transform the EU into a fair and prosperous society, with a modern, resource-efficient, and competitive economy, where there are no net emissions of greenhouse gases in 2050 and where economic growth is decoupled from resource use.
27. The EGD Circular Economy transformation consists of a mobilizing industrial strategy for a clean and circular economy with six key actions and aims to transform the industrial sector and all the value chains within 25 years from 2025 until 2050 into a sustainable model of inclusive growth by usying Circular Economy's potential for new activities and jobs.
28. The EU's Clean Industrial Deal (CID) shapes Packaging Policy and Circular Economy through its resource security policy and harmonization of circularity. European Legislation on Critical Raw Materials (Critical Raw Materials Act) and Circular Economy (Cirular Economy Act) function as catalysts for the CID's conceptualization of circularity and self-sufficiency on the road to makte Europe's industrial production more sustainable, speed-up decarbonization and enhance resource security.
29. The EU's New Circular Economy Action Plan (CEAP) describes Packaging Policy and Circular Economy in succession of the CEAP, while containing a policy of "cleaner, more competitive, and co-creative" ("Triple C Policy") after the EU's policy adjustment in order to react to the outcomes of the CEAP implementation report.
30. The European Strategy for Plastics in a Circular Economy, the so-called EU Plastics Strategy, comprehends Packaging Policy and Circular Economy in the light of a Plastics Industry Reformation Policy, i.e. rethinking and improving the European plastics industry via establishing a strategic vision and by laying the foundations to a new (circular) plastics economy, and a Plastics Value Chain Transformation, i.e. considering the various stages of a product in its way from "cradle to grave" or—in terms of a Circular Economy—"cradle to cradle".
31. The PPWR contains a compehensive regime of Packaging Policy and Circular Economy, which is accompanied accompanied by 13 annexes and subdivided into 188 recitals and 13 chapters consisting of 71 articles.
32. The PPWR contains four striking characteristics, which concern the PPWR's subject matter, packaging waste hierarchy, sustainability requirements, and extended packaging producer responsibility.
33. With the regulatory shift from a directive to a regulation, legal obligations under the PPWR are, in contrast to the PPWD, generally no longer addressed exclusively to the Member States as laid down in Article 288 para. 3 TFEU, but directly applicable according to Article 288 para. 2 sentence 2 TFEU, notably private entities addressed in a particular provision.
34. Article 1 para. 1 PPWR differentiates between two groups with different legal consequences, i.e. non-common requirements for packaging waste in regard to

EPR, collection, treatment, and recycling and common requirements for packaging to allow its placing on the market in regard to environmental sustainability and labelling.

35. According to Article 1 para. 1 PPWR, the regulation differentiates between packaging and packaging waste. The provision contains requirements for packaging in terms of environmental sustainability and labelling, to allow its placing on the market, and stipulates requirements for packaging waste in matters of EPR, packaging waste prevention including the reduction of unnecessary packaging and the re-use or reduction of packaging, the collection of packaging waste and its treatment encompassing the recycling of packaging waste. The distinction between packaging and packaging waste correlates with a diffentiated regime of legal consequences. While for packaging, the placing on the market is conceptualized as permissive requirement, the regulation follows an approach of reactive measures for packaging waste.
36. The term "life cycle of packaging", which is legally defined in Article 3 para. 1 subpara. 1 pt. 67 PPWR and referred to in Article 1 para. 1 PPWR, must be interpreted, behind the backdrop of the referral to packaging's design in Rec. 17 PPWR and consequently the packaging's purpose, from an objective perspective of a neutral third party with the necessary expertise, because otherwise—from a subjective perspective—a private entity, for instance the designer of the packaging, could decide on the temporal applicability of the PPWR.
37. Article 1 para. 3 PPWR differs from Article 1 para. 2 PPWD by declaring that the waste hierarchy of Article 4 WFD is applicable for packaging and packaging waste.
38. The PPWR formulates detailed specifications for the sustainability of packaging, including requirements for substances in packaging,[7] recyclable packaging,[8] minimum recycled content in plastic packaging,[9] biobased feedstock in plastic packaging,[10] compostable packaging,[11] packaging minimization,[12] and reusable packaging.[13]
39. The PPWR establishes basic rules for a European Extended Packaging Producer Responsibility.
40. The PPWR's obligations to register[14] (Article 39 para. 2 PPWR) and to apply for authorization[15] (Article 42 para. 1 PPWR) have vertical direct effect between the EU and the private entity concerned.

[7] Article 5 PPWR.

[8] Article 6 PPWR.

[9] Article 7 PPWR.

[10] Article 8 PPWR.

[11] Article 9 PPWR.

[12] Article 10 PPWR.

[13] Article 11 PPWR.

[14] Article 44 para. 2 sentence 1 PPWR.

[15] Article 47 para. 1 PPWR.

41. The PPWR's right of providers of online platforms to obtain certain information on the registration and to demand a self-certification of such producers directly from these producers[16] has horizontal direct effect between private entities.
42. The revision of European Packaging Law extends the regulatory density of EPR in the field of Packaging Policy and Circular Economy and introduces a European Extended Packaging Producer Responsibility.
43. The subject matter of European Extended Packaging Producer Responsibility is predominantely determined by Article 45 PPWR, which refers—similar to Article 7 para. 2 PPWD—to Article 8 and 8a WFD.
44. The administrative procedure of European Extended Packaging Producer Responsibility can be basically characterized as a two-tiered proceeding of registration[17] and authorization,[18] for which producers can or must—pursuant to the national law of the Member States—entrust a producer responsibility organization.[19]

7.2 Prospect

In the introduction, the question was raised, how the EU formulates and implements the European Green Deal agenda in the field of its Packaging Policy and Packaging Legislation to ensure the Circular Economy transition. Therefore, the EU's corresponding agenda-setting and instrument selection was evaluated in order to concretize and systematize the EU's objectives and measures. On this basis, the analysis has delivered several results, which highlight the characteristics of European Packaging Policy in the field of Circular Economy and thus indicate an answer to the initially raised question. Hence, it can be concluded that the EU acts based on the following policy characteristics:

Firstly, the EU's Packaging Policy in the field of Circular Economy is predetermined by the UN 2030 Agenda SDG 12 for sustainable consumption and production patterns and prospectively also will be affected by the UN Plastic Pollution Treaty. At the same time, the EU aspires to take over global leadership, especially through international fora, like the Global Alliance on Circular Economy and Resource Efficiency, the G7 or the G20, and is thus respectively involved in the global policy-making process through the European Commission's Green Diplomacy & Multilateralism Directorate and the Climate, Environment & Energy Diplomacy of the European External Action Service.

Secondly, European Packaging Policy and Circular Economy are forged under the participation and influence of the European Commission's Circular Economy Directorate according to its Strategic Plan 2020–2024 (Environment), the European

[16] Article 45 para. 4 PPWR.

[17] Article 44 PPWR.

[18] Article 47 PPWR.

[19] Article 46 PPWR.

Parliament's Committee on the Environment, Public Health, and Food Safety under the support of the European Parliamentary Research Service's Panel for the Future of Science and Technology, the think tanks of the European Environment Agency and its European Environment Information and Observation Network, and the Council of the European Union als European Environmental Governance Actor.

Thirdly, European Packaging Policy and Circular Economy are framed by the legal basis, basic principles, regulatory system and policy instruments of European Packaging Legislation. While either Article 114 TFEU (internal market) or Article 191 para. 1 TFEU (environment) can provide a legal basis, the relevant basic principles are the precautionary principle, the prevention principle, the rectification at source principle, and the polluter pays principle[20] and the environmental principles of integration and sustainability.[21] The regulatory system ensures legal coherence through policy alignment between Circular Economy law and Packaging law, especially based on interlinked governance mechanisms, such as the general rules of the WFD. Typical policy instruments to integrate and transfer the EU's Packaging Policy into secondary law are the waste hierarchy, bans, targets, information, and EPR.

Fourthly, European Packaging Policy and Circular Economy are conceptionalized through the European Green Deal's transformation policy and its roadmap for Circular Economy transformation, the Clean Industrial Deal's resource security policy and harmonization of circularity, the New Circular Economy Action Plan's "Triple C Policy" of "cleaner, more competitive, and co-creative", and the European Strategy for Plastics' policies of Plastic Industry Reformation and Plastic Value Chain Transformation.

Fifthly, the European Packaging Law Revision through the PPWR contains a compehensive regime of Packaging Policy and Circular Economy with four striking characteristics, which concern the PPWR's subject matter, packaging waste hierarchy, sustainability requirements and extended packaging producer responsibility.

Beyond these findings, the analysis contributes to the existing research on Packaging Policy and Circular Economy by concretizing, systematizing, and clarifying the Packaging Legislation of the EU under the European Green Deal during the different stages of the policy-making process. It hereby delivers a new framework for the assessment of existing policies and the development of new policies in the respective field. A guideline function may therefore be identified in the overall output of the analysis. The analysis may also serve as a source of information and explanatory comment for EU actors, who are involved in the implementation of European Packaging Policy. This may notably concern the transposition of European secondary law into the Member States' national law and the private sector adjustment to European secondary law requirements, especially through governance and compliance structures and strategies such as the Environmental Social Governance or the Corporate Social Responsibility of private entities.

[20] Article 191 para. 2 subpara. 1 sentence 2 TFEU.

[21] Article 11 TFEU, Article 37 CFR.

From a forward-looking perspective, the current state of European Packaging Policy suggests that the Circular Economy transition has entered a phase of regulatory consolidation rather than conceptual experimentation. Future developments are therefore likely to focus on the refinement, enforcement and integration of existing instruments, particularly in light of the forthcoming Circular Economy Act as enhanced basic legal framework and the increasing linkage between packaging regulation, industrial policy and resource security. Considering the perpetually ongoing Circular Economy transition process, a deepening and expansion of Packaging Policy ambitions and respective requirements can be expected in the future. The EU's challenge in this constellation and under the given preconditions will be complex. The EU will have to communicate, mediate, and manage Packaging Policy between multiple actors, notably with other states and international organizations in the global arena, with its Member States for the implementation into their national law, and with entities of private sector involvement regarding their backbone function to deliver on the Circular Economy transition at the end of the chain of policy implementation and obligation fulfilment. Furthermore, the EU will also have to develop new Packaging Policy approaches and concepts to address adequately the global and international dimension of the environmental and economical challenges for the Circular Economy transition to ensure an equilibrium of sustainability and prosperity. If the EU succeeds in this task, it is likely that its ambition to take over global leadership in the Circular Economy transition will be achievable. In this constellation, the EU could presumably benefit in its global position and exemplary function from an international spill-over effect and thus function as catalyser for a globally coordinated and effective system of transnational Circular Economy and mutually complementary international Packaging Policy, including the striking issue of single-use plastics.

Against this backdrop, the EU seems to be at a crossroads for the future development of Packaging Policy and Circular Economy. At this critical juncture, the direction taken in the coming years will largely determine whether the EU's ambitious regulatory architecture can be translated into a durable and effective transformation of production and consumption systems. The policy framework is now largely in place, with the European Green Deal, the PPWR, the Clean Industrial Deal and the imminent Circular Economy Act forming a dense and interlinked body of law and strategy. The decisive challenge therefore no longer lies primarily in norm creation, but in the consolidation, coordination and credible enforcement of existing rules under increasingly complex economic, geopolitical and societal conditions.

In this context, one of the central risks for the future development of EU Packaging Policy lies in the growing tension between regulatory ambition and implementation capacity. While harmonized and directly applicable rules promise legal certainty and internal market coherence, their practical execution depends on the administrative resources of Member States and the compliance structures of economic operators. Divergences in enforcement practices, infrastructure availability and market maturity may undermine the uniformity sought by EU legislation and risk creating de facto fragmentation despite formal harmonisation. In particular, insufficient recycling capacity, limited access to high-quality secondary raw materials or delays in digital reporting systems could weaken the effectiveness of circularity requirements and erode trust among regulated actors. Moreover, an overly rigid regulatory approach may generate resistance from industry or consumers if economic and social impacts are perceived as disproportionate or insufficiently mitigated. At the same time, the EU faces external risks that could significantly affect the trajectory of Packaging Policy and Circular Economy. Global competition for raw materials, volatile energy markets and geopolitical disruptions pose challenges to supply security and industrial competitiveness. In such an environment, circularity may be deprioritized in favor of short-term economic stabilization, particularly in times of crisis. There is also the risk that international regulatory divergence, especially in relation to packaging standards and waste management, could place EU companies at a competitive disadvantage if global partners do not pursue comparable levels of ambition. This underscores the importance of aligning internal regulation with external trade, diplomacy and development policies to prevent regulatory isolation.

Conversely, the current juncture also presents substantial opportunities for the EU to consolidate and extend its leadership in Circular Economy governance. If effectively implemented, the existing regulatory framework can create a genuinely integrated internal market for circular products and secondary raw materials, fostering innovation, investment and economies of scale. Packaging Policy, due to its cross-sectoral relevance and high visibility, has the potential to function as a catalyst for broader systemic change, influencing product design, logistics, consumer behavior and waste management practices far beyond the packaging sector itself. The increasing integration of circularity into industrial and competitiveness strategies further enhances the potential for synergies between environmental protection and economic value creation. In addition, the EU is well positioned to leverage its regulatory experience and market size to shape international norms and standards. By demonstrating that ambitious packaging regulation can coexist with industrial competitiveness and social acceptance, the Union may strengthen its normative power and promote regulatory convergence at the global level. This could be particularly significant in the context of emerging international agreements on plastic pollution and sustainable resource use, where the EU's internal legal framework may serve as a reference point for other jurisdictions. Such an international spill-over effect would not only reduce competitive asymmetries but also enhance the environmental effectiveness of circular policies on a global scale, leading by example for other nations and global actors to follow suit in fostering a truly Circular Economy.

Ultimately, the future of EU Packaging Policy and Circular Economy will depend on the Union's ability to navigate this crossroads with strategic coherence and institutional flexibility. Managing the risks of over-complexity, uneven implementation and external pressure will require continuous policy learning, stakeholder engagement and adaptive governance. At the same time, seizing the opportunities inherent in regulatory consolidation, market integration and global leadership could allow the EU to transform Packaging Policy into a cornerstone of a resilient, resource-efficient and competitive economic model. Whether the EU succeeds in this endeavour will be decisive for the credibility of its broader Circular Economy transition and for its capacity to reconcile sustainability, prosperity and strategic autonomy in the decades to come.

References

Adamowicz M (2022) Green deal, green growth and green economy as a means of support for attaining the sustainable development goals. Sustainability 14(10) 5901: 1–32
Alt M (2018) Ökodesign und Kreislaufwirtschaft. Kohärenz von Steuerungsansätzen zur Abfallvermeidung und "recyclinggerechtem Desgin" im Abfall- und Produktrecht am Beispiel von energieverbrauchsrelevanten Produkten. Nomos, Baden-Baden
Becker JP (2018) Cradle to Cradle als neue Philosophie der nachhaltigen Produktentwicklung. In: Scholz U, Pastoors S, Becker JP, Hofmann D, van Dun R (eds) Praxishandbuch Nachhaltige Produktentwicklung. Ein Leitfaden mit Tipps zur Entwicklung und Vermarktung nachhaltiger Produkte. Springer, Berlin, pp 31–38
Beckmann M (2023) Obhutspflicht und Warenvernichtungsverbot – Neue Instrumente einer nachhaltigen Kreislaufwirtschaft. In: Doumet J, Friedrich B, Lemperle I (eds) Kreislauf – Wirtschaft – Recht. Festschrift für Frank Petersen. Lexxion, Berlin, pp 113–132
Biermann F (2015) The rationale for a United Nations Environment Organization. In: Rechkemmer A (ed) UNEO – Towards an International Environment Organization. Approaches to a sustainable reform of global environmental governance. Nomos, Baden-Baden, pp 182–202
Borgmann-Prebil Y (2008) The rule of reason in European citizenship. Eur Law J 14:328–350
Brown ML (2012) Global environmental governance. Int Stud Rev 14:125–130
Bundela AK, Pandey KK (2022) The United Nations general assembly passes historic resolution to beat plastic pollution. Antr Sci 1:332–336
Bungard D (2023) EU-Green Deal und Auswirkungen auf den Mittelstand in der Entsorgungs- und Recyclingwirtschaft. In: Doumet J, Friedrich B, Lemperle I (eds) Kreislauf – Wirtschaft – Recht. Festschrift für Frank Petersen. Lexxion, Berlin, pp 243–252
Burns C, Tobin P (2018) The limits of ambitious environmental policy in times of crisis. In: Adelle C, Biedenkopf K, Torney D (eds) European Union external environmental policy. Rules, regulation and governance beyond borders. Springer Nature, Cham, pp 319–336
Calliess C (2022a) Art. 5 EUV. In: Calliess C, Ruffert M (eds) EUV/AEUV, 6th edn. C.H. Beck, München
Calliess C (2022b) Art. 191 AEUV. In: Calliess C, Ruffert M (eds) EUV/AEUV, 6th edn. C.H. Beck, München
Calliess C, Tuncel E (2023) The Role of Article 11 TFEU in the Greening of the ECB's Monetary Policy. Ger. Law J. 24 First View: 1–29
Canton H (2021) United Nations industrial development organizations – UNIDO. In: Canton H (ed) The Europa directory of international organizations, 23rd edn. Routledge/Milton Park, Abingdon, Oxon, pp 365–367
Caspersen O (1999) The European environment agency. Glob Environ Change 9:71–75
Circular Plastics Alliance (2019) Declaration of the Circular Plastics Alliance of 16.07.2019, https://ec.europa.eu/docsroom/documents/36361

R. H. D. Reimer, *Packaging Policy and Circular Economy*, Law for Professionals, https://doi.org/10.1007/978-3-032-27081-8

Citaristi I (2022) United Nations industrial development organizations – UNIDO. In: Canton H (ed) The Europa directory of international organizations, 24th edn. Routledge/Milton Park, Abingdon, Oxon, pp 375–378

Clift R, Martin G, Mair S (2022) Sustainability and the circular economy. In: Teodosiu C, Fiore S, Hospido A (eds) Assessing progress towards sustainability. Frameworks, tools and case studies. Elsevier, Amsterdam, pp 35–56

Compagnoni M (2022) Is Extended Producer Responsibility living up to expectations? A systematic literature review focusing on electronic waste. J Clean Prod 367:133101

Council of the European Union (2018) Delivering on the EU Action Plan for the Circular Economy, Council Conclusions of 25.6.2019, 10447/18, https://www.consilium.europa.eu/media/35781/st10447-en18.pdf

Council of the European Union (2018) Eco-innovation: enabling the transition towards a circular economy, Council Conclusions of 18.12.2017, 15811/17, https://data.consilium.europa.eu/doc/document/ST-15811-2017-INIT/en/pdf.

Council of the European Union (2019) An EU Industrial Policy Stratetgy: a Vision for 2030, Council Conclusions of 27.5.2019, 9706/19, https://data.consilium.europa.eu/doc/document/ST-9706-2019-INIT/en/pdf

Council of the European Union (2019) More circularity – Transition to a sustainable society, Council Conclusions of 4.10.2019, 12791/19, https://www.consilium.europa.eu/media/40928/st12791-en19.pdf

Council of the European Union (2019) The 8th Environment Action Programme – Turning the Trends Together, Council Conclusions of 4.10.2019, 12795/19, https://www.consilium.europa.eu/media/40927/st12795-2019.pdf

Council of the European Union (2019) Towards an ever more sustainable Union by 2030, Council Conclusions of 9.4.2019, 8286/19, https://data.consilium.europa.eu/doc/document/ST-8286-2019-INIT/en/pdf

Council of the European Union (2020) Draft Council conclusions on Making the Recovery Circular and Green of 11.12.2020, 13852/20, https://data.consilium.europa.eu/doc/document/ST-13852-2020-INIT/en/pdf.

Council of the European Union (2025) General Secretariat of the Council (GSC) organisation chart (16 January 2026), https://www.consilium.europa.eu/media/eimlovjd/gsc-organisation-chart-en.pdf

Dalhammer C (2023) Extended producer responsibility. In: Faure M (ed) Elgar Encyclopedia of environmental law. Edward Elgar Publishing, Cheltenham, pp 208–218

Dammann S, Gee D (2011) Science into policy: the European environment agency. In: Lentsch J, Weingart P (eds) The politics of scientific advice. Institutional design for quality assurance. Cambridge, Cambridge University Press, pp 238–258

Dauses MA (1998) Information der Verbraucher in der Rechtsprechung des EuGH. RIW 12:750–757

Denta SM (2022) Preventing Plastic pollution with a global plastic treaty and public-private partnership for the climate. EPPPL 17:211–220

Desai BH (2014) International environmental governance. Towards UNEPO. Brill, Leiden

Downie DL, Levy MA (2000) The UN environment programme at a turning point: options for change. In: Chasek PS (ed) The global environment in the twenty-first century: prospects for international cooperation. United Nations University Press, Tokyo, pp 355–377

Elia V, Gnoni MG, Tornese F (2015) Designing Pay-As-You-Throw schemes in municipal waste management services: a holistic approach. Waste Manage 44:188–195

Engelmann M (2024a) Mehrwegquoten für Industrie- und Gewerbeverpackungen in Art. 29 PPWR. AbfallR 4:159–171

Engelmann M (2024b) Verpackungs- und Produktverbote in der EU-Verpackungsverordnung (PPWR). Eine kritische Analyse und Bewertung. AbfallR 5:216–230

Epiney A (2018) Art. 191. In: Vedder C, Heintschel von Heinegg W (eds) Europäisches Unionsrecht, 2nd edn. C.H. Beck, München

Epiney A (2019) Umweltrecht der Europäischen Union, 4th edn. Nomos, Baden-Baden

European Commission (2015) Closing the loop – An EU action plan for the Circular Economy, Communiucation of 2.12.2015, COM(2015) 614 final
European Commission (2018) A European Strategy for Plastics in a Circular Economy, Communication of 16.1.2018, COM(2018) 28 final
European Commission (2018) Annexes 1 to 3 to the Communication of a European Strategy for Plastics in a Circular Economy, Communiucation of 16.1.2018, COM(2018) 28 final, Annexes 1 to 3
European Commission (2018) Commission Staff Working Document accompanying the document A European Strategy for Plastics in a Circular Economy, Commission Staff Working Document of 16.1.2018, SWD(2018) 16 final
European Commission (2019) Annex to the Communication on Closing the loop – An EU action plan for the Circular Economy, Communiucation of 2.12.2015, COM(2015) 614 final, Annex 1
European Commission (2019) Annex to the Communication on the European Green Deal, Communiucation of 11.12.2019, COM(2019) 640 final, Annex
European Commission (2019) Preventing plastic waste in Europe, Report No 2/2019 of 3.6.2019, https://www.eea.europa.eu/publications/preventing-plastic-waste-in-europe
European Commission (2019) Report on the implementation of the Circular Economy Action Plan, Report of 4.3.2019. COM(2019) 190 final
European Commission (2019) The European Green Deal, Communiucation of 11.12.2019, COM(2019) 640 final
European Commission (2019) Paving the way for a circular economy: insights on status and potentials, Report No 11/2019 of 1.10.2019, https://www.eea.europa.eu/publications/circular-economy-in-europe-insights
European Commission (2020) A new Circular Economy Action Plan. For a cleaner and more competitive Europe, Communication of 11.3.2020, COM(2020) 98 final
European Commission (2020) A New Industrial Strategy for Europe, Communication of 10.3.2020, COM(2020) 102 final
European Commission (2020) Leading the way to a global circular economy: state of play and outlook, Commission Staff Working Document of 11.03.2020, SWD(2020) 100 final
European Commission (2020) Strategic plan 2020-2024 – Environment, Ref. Ares(2020)4902415 – 18/09/2020, https://commission.europa.eu/publications/strategic-plan-2020-2024-environment_en
European Commission (2020) Resource efficiency and the circular economy in Europe 2019 – even more from less. An overview of the policies, approaches and targets of 32 European countries, Report No 26/2019 of 1.4.2020, https://www.eea.europa.eu/publications/even-more-from-less
European Commission (2020) The plastic waste trade in the circular economy, Report of 28.10.2020, https://www.eea.europa.eu/en/analysis/publications/the-plastic-waste-trade-in
European Commission (2021) Updating the 2020 New Industrial Strategy: Building a stronger Single Market for Europe's recovery, Communication of 5.5.2021, COM(2021) 350 final
European Commission (2021) Plastics, the circular economy and Europe's environment – A priority for action, Report No 18/2020 of 28.1.2021, https://www.eea.europa.eu/publications/plastics-the-circular-economy-and/
European Commission (2022) Annexes 1 to 13 to the Proposal for a Regulation of the European Parliament and of the Council on packaging and packaging waste, amending Regulation (EU) 2019/1020 and Directive (EU) 2019/904, and repealing Directive 94/62/EC of 30.11.2022, COM(2022) 677 final Annexes 1 to 13
European Commission (2022) Annual activity report 2021 – Environment, Ref. Ares(2022)2419650 – 31/03/2022, https://commission.europa.eu/publications/annual-activity-report-2021-environment_en
European Commission (2022) Commission work programme 2023. A Union standing firm and united, Communication of 18.10.2022, COM(2022) 548 final
European Commission (2022) EU Strategy for Sustainable and Circular Textiles, Communication of 30.3.2022, COM(2022) 141 final

European Commission (2022) Executive Summary of the Impact Assessment Report, Accompanying the document Proposal for a Regulation of the European Parliament and of the Council on packaging and packaging waste, amending Regulation (EU) 2019/1020 and Directive (EU) 2019/904, and repealing Directive 94/62/EC, Staff Working Document of 30.11.2022, SWD(2022) 385 final

European Commission (2022) Impact Assessment Report, Accompanying the document Proposal for a Regulation of the European Parliament and of the Council on packaging and packaging waste, amending Regulation (EU) 2019/1020 and Directive (EU) 2019/904, and repealing Directive 94/62/EC, Staff Working Document of 30.11.2022, SWD(2022) 384 final, Part 1/2

European Commission (2022) Impact Assessment Report, Accompanying the document Proposal for a Regulation of the European Parliament and of the Council on packaging and packaging waste, amending Regulation (EU) 2019/1020 and Directive (EU) 2019/904, and repealing Directive 94/62/EC, Staff Working Document of 30.11.2022, SWD(2022) 384 final, Part 2/2

European Commission (2022) Management plan 2022 – Environment, Ref. Ares(2022)342601 – 17/01/2022, https://commission.europa.eu/publications/management-plan-2022-environment_en

European Commission (2022) Proposal for a Directive of the European Parliament and of the Council concerning urban wastewater treatment (recast) of 26.10.2022, COM(2022) 541 final

European Commission (2022) Proposal for a Regulation of the European Parliament and of the Council on packaging and packaging waste, amending Regulation (EU) 2019/1020 and Directive (EU) 2019/904, and repealing Directive 94/62/EC of 30.11.2022, COM(2022) 677 final

European Commission (2023) Circular economy for textiles: taking responsibility to reduce, reuse and recycle textile waste and boosting markets for used textiles, press release of 5.7.2023, https://ec.europa.eu/commission/presscorner/detail/en/ip_23_3635

European Commission (2023) Environment – organisation chart, https://commission.europa.eu/about-european-commission/departments-and-executive-agencies/environment_en

European Commission (2023) Conditions and pathways for sustainable and circular consumption in Europe, Report of 13.6.2023, https://www.eea.europa.eu/en/analysis/publications/conditions-and-pathways-for-sustainable

European Commission (2023) Investigating Europe's secondary raw material markets, Report No 12/2022 of 26.1.2023, https://www.eea.europa.eu/publications/investigating-europes-secondary-raw-material

European Commission (2023) Pathways towards circular plastics in Europe – good practice examples from countries, business and citizens, Report of 20.2.2023, https://www.eea.europa.eu/en/analysis/publications/pathways-towards-circular-plastics

European Commission (2023) Tracking waste prevention progress – A narrative-based waste prevention monitoring framework at the EU level, Report No 2/2023 of 17.5.2023, https://www.eea.europa.eu/publications/tracking-waste-prevention-progress

European Commission (2025) The Clean Industrail Deal: A roadmap for competitiveness and decarbonization, Communication of 26.2.2025, COM(2025) 85 final

European Economic and Social Committee (2023) Opinion on the proposal for a Directive of the European Parliament and of the Council concerning urban wastewater treatment of 22.2.2023, 2023/C 146/06, OJ C 146/35, 27.4.203, p. 35.

European Environment Agency (2020) Biodegradable and compostable plastics – challenges and opportunities, Report of 27.8.2020, https://www.eea.europa.eu/en/analysis/publications/biodegradable-and-compostable-plastics-challenges-and-opportunities

European External Action Service (2020) EU-India: Partners for Circular Economy & Resource Efficiency, Broschure of 28.09.2020, https://www.eeas.europa.eu/sites/default/files/rei_brochure_updated_v10_optimized.pdf

European External Action Service (2021) EU-Gulf Cooperation Council (GCC) Dialogue on Economic Diversification. Gulf Cooperation Council (GCC) Countries. Study on Circular Economy developments in the GCC region and opportunities for collaboration with the

European Union, Report of 1.4.2021, https://www.eeas.europa.eu/sites/default/files/documents/Circular%20economy%20in%20GCC%20Report%202021%2004.pdf
European Parliament (2020) Report on the New Circular Economy Action Plan of 28.1.2021, 2020/2077(INI), A9-0008/2021, PE652.387v03-00
European Parliament (2022) Draft Report on the proposal for a regulation of the European Parliament and of the Council amending Regulation (EC) No 1272/2008 of the European Parliament and of the Council on classification, labelling and packaging of substances and mixtures of 5.4.2023, COM(2022)0748, C9-0433/2022, 2022/0432(COD), PE745.493v01-00
European Parliament (2022) Resource efficiency and circular economy, Fact sheet of 1.9.2022, https://www.europarl.europa.eu/factsheets/en/sheet/76/resource-efficiency-and-the-circular-economy
European Parliament (2023) Draft report on the proposal for a regulation of the European Parliament and of the Council on packaging and packaging waste, amending Regulation (EU) 2019/1020 and Directive (EU) 2019/904, and repealing Directive 94/62/EC of 11.4.2023, COM(2022)0677, C9-0400/2022, 2022/0396(COD), PE742.297v01-00
European Parliament and Council of the European Union (2013) Decision No 1386/2013/EU of the European Parliament and of the Council of 20 November 2013 on a General Union Action Programme to 2020 "Living well, within the limits of our planet", OJ L 354, 28.12.2013, p. 171, https://eur-lex.europa.eu/legal-content/EN/TXT/?uri=CELEX:32013D1386
European Parliament and Council of the European Union (2022) Decision (EU) 2022/591 of the European Parliament and of the Council of 6 April 2022 on General Union Environment Action Programme to 2030, OJ L 114, 12.4.2022, p. 22, https://eur-lex.europa.eu/legal-content/EN/TXT/?uri=CELEX%3A32022D0591
European Parliamentary Research Service (2017) Towards a circular economy – Waste management in the EU, Study PE 581.913 of 25.9.2017, https://www.europarl.europa.eu/stoa/en/document/EPRS_STU(2017)581913
European Parliamentary Research Service (2021) EU climate action policy: Responding to the global emergency, Study PE 689.378 of 18.3.2021, https://www.europarl.europa.eu/thinktank/en/document/EPRS_STU(2021)689378
European Parliamentary Research Service (2021) Meeting the Green Deal objectives by alignment of technology and behaviour, Study PE 656.337 of 9.7.2021, https://www.europarl.europa.eu/stoa/en/document/EPRS_STU(2021)656337
European Parliamentary Research Service (2022) The Green Deal ambition: Technology, creativity and the arts for environmental sustainability, Study PE 729.513 of 31.5.2022, https://www.europarl.europa.eu/stoa/en/document/EPRS_STU(2022)729513
European Parliamentary Research Service (2023) Revision of the Packaging and Packaging Waste Directive, Briefing PE 745.707 of 31.3.2023, https://www.europarl.europa.eu/thinktank/en/document/EPRS_BRI(2023)745707
European Topic Centre on Circular Economy and Resource Use (2022) Flexible plastics in Europe's circular economy, Report 4/2022 of 28.9.2022, https://www.eionet.europa.eu/etcs/etc-ce/products/etc-ce-products/etc-ce-report-4-2022-flexible-plastics-in-europe2019s-circular-economy.
European Topic Centre on Circular Economy and Resource Use (2023) Analysis of the circular material use rate and the doubling target, Report 2023/6 of 25.4.2023, https://www.eionet.europa.eu/etcs/etc-ce/products/etc-ce-report-2023-6-analysis-of-the-circular-material-use-rate-and-the-doubling-target
European Topic Centre on Circular Economy and Resource Use (2023) Pathways to circular plastics in Europe: Good examples from countries, business and citizens, Report 2023/1 of 20.2.2023, https://www.eionet.europa.eu/etcs/etc-ce/products/etc-ce-report-2023-2-the-fate-of-eu-plastic-waste.
European Topic Centre on Circular Economy and Resource Use (2023) The fate of EU plastic waste, Report 2023/2 of 20.2.2023, https://www.eionet.europa.eu/etcs/etc-ce/products/etc-ce-report-2023-2-the-fate-of-eu-plastic-waste
Flanderka F (2014) § 23 KrWG. In: Brandt A, Deifuß-Kruse D, Jahn C (eds) Kreislaufwirtschaftsgesetz. Kommentar. Kohlhammer, Stuttgart
Förstner U, Köster S (2018) Umweltschutztechnik, 9th edn. Springer Vieweg, Berlin

Gaur A, Gurjar SK, Chaudhary S (2022) Circular system of resource recovery and reverse logistics approach: key to zero waste and zero landfill. In: Hussain C, Hait S (eds) Advanced organic waste management. Sustainable practices and approaches. Elsevier, Amsterdam, pp 365–380

Gharfalkar M, Court R, Campbell C, Zulfiqur A, Hillier G (2015) Analysis of waste hierarchy in the European waste directive 2008/98/EC. Waste Manage 39:305–313

Giesler M, Veresiu E (2014) Creating the responsible consumer: moralistic governance regimes and consumer subjectivity. J Consum Res 41:840–857

Ginsberg RH (2010) Demystifying the European Union. The enduring logic of regional integration, 2nd edn. Rowman & Littlefield Publishers, Plymouth

Governing Council of the United Nations Environment Programme (1985) Establishment of a Committee of Permanent Representatives, UNEP/GC.13/2 (23 May 1985)

Governing Council of the United Nations Environment Programme (2013) Proceedings of the Governing Council/Global Ministerial Environment Forum at its first universal session, UNEP/GC.27/17 (12 March 2013)

Gupta J (2023) E-waste: policies and legislations for a sustainable green growth. In: Singh P, Verma P, Ahamad A, Batalhão ACS (eds) Waste management and resource recycling in the developing world. Elsevier, Amsterdam, pp 253–270

Hadfield A, Fiott D (2014) Relations with the rest of the world: from chaos to consolidation? JCMS 52:170–185

Halmaghi E-E (2016) Einvironmental action programmes of the European Union – programmes supporting the sustainable development strategy of the European Union. Scie Bull 21:87–90

Hayes-Renshaw F, Wallace H (2006) The council of ministers, 2nd edn. Palgrave Macmillan, Basingstoke

Heine D, Faure MG, Dominioni G (2020) The polluter-pays principle in climate change law: an economic appraisal. Clim Law 10:94–115

Heussner K (2007) Informationssysteme im Europäischen Verwaltungsverbund. Mohr Siebeck, Tübingen

Hilbert P (2022) Die Informationsfunktion von Parlamenten. Zugleich ein Beitrag zur demokratischen Bedeutung des Europäischen Parlaments. Mohr Siebeck, Tübingen

Homann V, Franßen G (2024) Geplante und bestehende Regulierungen in Bezug auf primäres und sekundäres Mikroplastik. StoffR 21:10–19

Hřebíček J (2003) Globale Umweltinformationssysteme im internationalen Maßstab. In: Kramer M, Brauweiler J, Helling (eds) Internationales Umweltmanagement, Bd. II: Umweltmanagementinstrumente und -systeme. Gabler, Wiesbaden, pp. 53–75

Huck W (2022) Sustainable development goals. Article-by-Article Commentary. Nomos, Baden-Baden

Huhta K, Kalimo H, Soininen N, Vesa S (2025) EU's clean industrial deal: a risk or an opportunity for sustainability? EEELR 34:95–105

Jacobya W, Hopkin J (2020) From lever to club? Conditionality in the European Union during the financial crisis. J Eur Public Policy 27:1157–1177

Johnstone N, Brown Z (2014) Better the devil you throw: experience and support for pay-as-you-throw waste charges. Environ Sci Policy 38:132–142

Junankar N (2023) Plastic pollution treaty way foreward. In: Krantzberg G, Jetoo S, Grover VI, Babel S (eds) Plastic pollution. Nature based solutions and effective governance. Taylor & Francis/Milton Park, Abingdon, Oxon, pp 218–224

Kachur M, Oehlmann C (2023) Ein echter Binnenmarkt für den Verpackungskreislauf? EU-Kommission legt erstmals Vorschlag für eine Verpackungsverordnung vor, AbfallR 22:19–31

Kahl W (2018) Art. 5 EUV. In: Streinz R (ed) EUV/AEUV, 3rd edn. C.H. Beck, München

Kahl W, Gärditz KF (2021) Umweltrecht, 12th edn, C.H. Beck, München

Käller A (2019) Art. 191 AEUV. In: Schwarze J, Becker U, Hatje A, School J (eds) EU-Kommentar, 4th edn. Nomos, Baden-Baden

Kalmykova Y, Sadagopan M, Rosado L (2018) Circular economy – From review of theories and practices to development of implementation tools. Resour Conserv Recycl 135:190–201

Kern F, Sharp H, Hachmann S (2020) Governing the second deep transition towards a circular economy: How rules emerge, align and diffuse. Environ Innov Soc Transit 37:171–186
Kingston S, Heyvaert V, Čavoški A (2017) European environmental law. Cambridge University Press, Cambridge
Kloepfer M (2016) Umweltrecht, 4th edn. C.H. Beck, München
Kosek K, Luczkiewicz A, Fudala-Książek S, Jankowska K, Szopińska M, Svahn O, Tränckner J, Kaiser A, Langas V, Björklund E (2020) Implementation of advanced micropollutants removal technologies in wastewater treatment plants (WWTPs) – examples and challenges based on selected EU countries. Environ Sci Policy 112:213–226
Kosior E, Crescenzi I (2020) Solutions to the plastic waste problem on land and in the oceans. In: Letcher TM (ed) Plastic waste and recycling. Environmental impact, societal issues, prevention, and solutions. Academic Press, London, pp 415–446
Kozień A (2021) The principle of sustainable development as the basis for weighing the public interest and individual interest in the scope of the cultural heritage protection law in the European Union. Sustainability 13(3985):1–17
Krämer L (2012) Giving a voice to the environment by challenging the practice of integrating environmental requirements into other EU policies. In: Kingston S (ed) European perspectives on environmental law and governance. Routledge/Milton Park, Abingdon, Oxon, pp 83–101
Krämer L (2015) Art. 191 AEUV. In: von der Groeben H, Schwarze J, Hatje A (eds) Europäisches Unionsrecht, 7th edn. Nomos, Baden-Baden
Kropp O (2024) Kreislaufwirtschaft und Chemikalienrecht. AbfallR 23:259–266
Langlet D, Mahmoudi S (2016) EU Environmental Law and Policy. Oxford University Press, Oxford
Lanzini P (2017) Responsible citizens and sustainable consumer behavior. New interpretative frameworks. Routledge, Milton Park, Abingdon, Oxon
Leisner W (1991) Der mündige Verbraucher in der Rechtsprechung des EuGH. EuZW 16:498–504
Lewis J (2007) The council of the European Union. In: Cini M (ed) European Union politics, 2nd edn. Oxford University Press, Oxford, pp 154–174
Lewis J (2022) The committee of permanent representatives: integrating interests and the logics of action. In: Hodson D, Puetter W, Saurugger S, Peterson J (eds) The institutions of the European Union, 5th edn. Oxford University Press, Oxford
Lindhout PE, van den Broek B (2014) The polluter pays principle: guidelines for cost recovery and burden sharing in the case law of the European Court of Justice. Utrecht Law Rev 10:46–59
Loschwitz J (2023) Obhutspflichten im Abfallrecht zwischen Anspruch und Wirklichkeit. In: Doumet J, Friedrich B, Lemperle I (eds) Kreislauf – Wirtschaft – Recht. Festschrift für Frank Petersen. Lexxion, Berlin, pp 75–112
Lubowiecki-Vikuk A, Dabrowska A, Machnik A (2021) Responsible consumer and lifestyle: sustainability insights. Sustain Prod Consum 25:91–101
Luken RA, Navratil J (2004) A programmatic review of UNIDO/UNEP national cleaner production centres. J Clean Prod 12:195–205
Martens M (2010) Voice or loyalty? The evolution of the European Environment Agency (EEA). JCMS 48:881–901
Mazur-Wierzbicka E (2021) Circular economy: advancement of European Union countries. ESEU 33, 111: 1–15.
Mhatre P, Panchal R, Singh A, Bibyan S (2021) A systematic literature review on the circular economy initiatives in the European Union. Sustain Prod Consum 26:187–202
Migliore M, Talamo C, Pagani G (2020) Strategies for circular economy and cross-sectoral exchanges for sustainable building products. Preventing and recycling waste. Springer, Cham
Moraga G, Huysveld S, Mathieux F, Blengini GA, Alaerts L, Van Acker K, de Meester S, Dewulf J (2019) Circular economy indicators: what do they measure? Resour Conserv Recycl 146:452–461
Moses SR, Piehl S, Ramsperger AFRM, Löder M, Laforsch C (2019) Plastik im aquatischen Ökosystem. In: Jaeckel L (ed) Ressourcen im globalen Kontext. Schutz und nachhaltige Nutzung. Mohr Siebeck, Tübingen, pp 93–106

Najam A, Papa M, Taiyab N (2006) Global environmental governance. A reform Agenda. International Institute for Sustainable Development, Winnipeg

Nash J, Bosso C (2013) Extended producer responsibility in the united states: full speed ahead? J Ind Ecol 17:175–185

Nedergard P (2007) European Union administration: legitimacy and efficiency. Martinus Nijhoff Publishers, Leiden

Nettesheim M (44th Update May 2011) Art. 191 AEUV. In: Grabitz E, Hilf M, Nettesheim M, Recht der Europäischen Union. C.H. Beck, München

Neves M (2021) Constitutionalism and the paradox of principles and rules. Between the hydra and hercules. Oxford University Press, Oxford

O'Connor M (1997) The internalisation of environmental costs: implementing the Polluter Pays principle in the European Union. IJEP 7:450–482

OECD (2022) Global Plastics Outlook. Economic Drivers, Environmental Impacts and Policy Options, 22 February 2022, https://www.oecd-ilibrary.org/environment/global-plastics-outlook_de747aef-en

Olatayo KI, Mativenga PT, Marnewick AL (2022) Does policy on plastic waste support higher waste management hierarchy options? Recycling 7(36):1–23

Peno M (2019) Philosophy of punishment: normative models and construction of legal systems. Zbornik PFZ 69:411–432

Petersen F (2022) Die Produktverantwortung im Kreislaufwirtschaftsrecht. NVwZ 13:921–930

Petersen F, Friedrich B (2021) Die Novellierung des Kreislaufwirtschaftsgesetzes 2020. NVwZ 1:1–10

Petersen F, Massow M (2023) Die EU-Ökodesign-Verordnung und das "Warenvernichtungsverbot" – Gefährdet die "nachhaltige Produktpolitik" die Kreislaufwirtschaft? ZUR 2:67–77

Pires A, Martinho G (2019) Waste hierarchy index for circular economy in waste management. Waste Manage 95:298–305

Proelss A (2016) Principles of EU environmental law: an appraisal. In: Nakanishi Y (ed) Contemporary issues in environmental law. The EU and Japan. Springer, Tokyo, pp 29–46

Proelss A (2023) Vom Verursacher- zum Nachhaltigkeitsprinzip: Wo steht das Umweltvölkergewohnheitsrecht? In: Gesellschaft für Umweltrecht (ed) Dokumentation zur 1. Digitalen Sondertagung der Gesellschaft für Umweltrecht e.V. 2022. Umweltvölkerrecht: heute und morgen. Erich Schmidt Verlag, Berlin, pp 25–54

Puente C (2014) Historical evolution of conditionality criteria in external relations of the EU with CEEC. From the cold war to the accession: an insider's perspective. RJEA 14:56–77

Reimer RHD (2022) Die Abfallhierarchie im Verpackungsrecht. Zur Wiederverwendung als Maßnahmenkategorie sui generis und zum verpackungsrechtlichen Gleichrangigkeitsprinzip. EurUP 2:165–176

Reimer RHD (2023) Grundstrukturen der kreislaufwirtschaftsrechtlichen Obhutspflicht, AbfallR 22:0 31–43.

Reßing M (2009) Prinzipien als Normen mit zwei Geltungsebenen. Zur Unterscheidung von Regeln und Prinzipien, ARSP 95:28–48

Ripoll Servant A (2018) The European Parliament. Palgrave, Basingstoke

Santiso C (2003) Sisyphus in the castle: improving European Union strategies for democracy promotion and governance conditionality. EJDR 15:1–28

Schönfelder L, Mühlmann F, Stahnke L (2025) Aktuelle Diskussionen und Tendenzen zur Umesetzung der neuen Kommunalabwasserrichtlinie in das deutsche Recht. StoffR 22:189–198

Schumacher T (2012) Conditionality, differentiation, regionality and the 'New' ENP in the light of arab revolts. In: Barbé E, Herranz-Surrallés A (eds) The challenge of differentiation in euro-mediterranean relations. Flexible regional cooperation or fragmentation. Routledge, Milton Park, Abingdon, Oxon, pp 142–158

Schwind MP (2017) Netzwerke im Europäischen Verwaltungsrecht. Ein Beitrag zu Theorie und Dogmatik der Behördenkoordination in der EU. Mohr Siebeck, Tübingen

Scotford E (2017) Environmental principles and the evolution of environmental law. Hart Publishing, Oxford and Portland, Oregon

Sieckmann J (2011) Prinzipien, ideales Sollen und normative Argumente. ARSP 97:178–197
Sin LT, Tueen BS (2023) Plastics and sustainability. Practical approaches. Elsevier, Amsterdam
Smith KR (2010) What's cooking? A brief update. Energy Sustain Dev 14:251–252
Sohn LB (1973) The Stockholm declaration on the human environment. HIJL 14:424–515
Spence D (2004) The European Commission's external service. PPA 19:61–76
Steenmans K, Ulfbeck V (2023) Fostering the circular economy through private law: Perspectives from the extended producer responsibility concept. Resour Conserv Recycl 195(107016):1–2
Stöfen-O'Brien A (2022) Common but differentiated responsibilities as a guiding principle towards a potential international treaty on plastic. In: Kraska J, Long R, Nordquist MH (eds) Peaceful maritime engagement in East Asia and the Pacific Region. Brill Nijhoff, Leiden, Boston, pp 370–386
Streinz R (2018) Art. 5 EUV. In: Streinz R (ed) EUV/AEUV, 3rd edn. C.H. Beck, München
Tömmel I (2014) Das politische System der EU, 4th edn. De Gruyter, München
Torney D, Davis Cross MK (2018) Environmental and climate diplomacy: building coalitions through persuasion. In: Adelle C, Biedenkopf K, Torney D (eds) European Union external environmental policy. Rules, regulation and governance beyond borders. Palgrave, Basingstoke, pp 39–58
United Nations (1972) Report of the United Nations Conference on the human environment, Stockholm, 5–16 June 1972, A/CONF.48/14/Rev. 1 (United Nations publication, Sales No. E.73.II.A.14)
United Nations (2012) Agenda item 10 of the United Nations Conference on Sustainable Development, Rio de Janeiro, 20–22 June 2012, A/CONF.216/L.1
United Nations Environment Assembly (2014) Marine plastic debris and microplastics, UNEP/EA.1/Res.6 (2014)
United Nations Environment Assembly (2014) Proceedings of the United Nations Environment Assembly of the United Nations Environment Programme at its first session, Nairobi, 23–27 June 2014, UNEP/EA.1/10 (2 September 2014)
United Nations Environment Assembly (2016) Marine plastic litter and microplastics, UNEP/EA.2/Res.11 (2016)
United Nations Environment Assembly (2017) Marine litter and microplastics, UNEP/EA.3/Res.7 (2017)
United Nations Environment Assembly (2019) Addressing single-use plastic products pollution, UNEP/EA.4/Res.9 (28 March 2019)
United Nations Environment Assembly (2019) Compilation of United Nations Environment Assembly resolutions on marine litter and microplastics, Ad hoc open-ended expert group on marine litter and microplastics, Third meeting Bangkok, 18–22 November 2019, UNEP/AHEG/2019/3/INF/2 (29 October 2019)
United Nations Environment Assembly (2019) Innovative pathways to achieve sustainable consumption and production, UNEP/EA.4/Res.1 (28 March 2019)
United Nations Environment Assembly (2019) Marine plastic litter and microplastics, UNEP/EA.4/Res.6 (2019)
United Nations Environment Assembly (2019) Proceedings of the United Nations Environment Assembly at its fourth session, Nairobi, 11–15 March 2019, UNEP/EA.4/2 (22 March 2019)
United Nations Environment Assembly (2022) End plastic pollution: towards an international legally binding instrument, UNEP/EA.5/Res.14 (7 March 2022)
United Nations Environment Programme (2019) Addressing Marine Plastics: A Roadmap to a Circular Economy, Roadmap (2019), https://wedocs.unep.org/handle/20.500.11822/32533
United Nations Environment Programme (2019) Addressing Marine Plastics: A Systemic Approach. Recommendations for Actions, Report (2 December 2019), https://wedocs.unep.org/handle/20.500.11822/31642.
United Nations Environment Programme (2019) New Plastics Economy Global. Commitment 2019 – Progress Report, Report (28 October 2019), https://wedocs.unep.org/handle/20.500.11822/30609

United Nations Environment Programme (2019) The Role of Packaging Regulations and Standards in Driving the Circular Economy, Report (13 November 2019), https://wedocs.unep.org/20.500.11822/30736
United Nations Environment Programme (2020) Single-use Plastic Bags and their Alternatives. Recommendations from Life Cycle Assessments, Report (5 March 2020), https://wedocs.unep.org/handle/20.500.11822/31932
United Nations Environment Programme (2021) Addressing Single-Use Plastic Products Pollution using a Life Cycle Approach, Report (30 June 2021), https://wedocs.unep.org/handle/20.500.11822/35109
United Nations Environment Programme (2021) Drowning in Plastics. Marine Litter and Plastic Waste Vital Graphics, Report (21 October 2021), https://wedocs.unep.org/handle/20.500.11822/36964
United Nations Environment Programme (2021) From Pollution to Solution. A Global Assessment of Marine Litter and Plastic Pollution, Report (21 November 2021), https://wedocs.unep.org/bitstream/handle/20.500.11822/36965/POLSOLSum.pdf?sequence=24&isAllowed=y
United Nations Environment Programme (2021) Tackling Plastic Pollution: Legislative Guide for the Regulation of Single-Use Plastic Products, Report (6 April 2021), https://wedocs.unep.org/handle/20.500.11822/34570
United Nations Environment Programme (2022) Concept Note – Global Alliance on Circular Economy and Resource Efficiency (GACERE): Towards Just Transitions (July 2022), https://wedocs.unep.org/handle/20.500.11822/40298
United Nations Environment Programme (2022) Single-use Supermarket Food Packaging and its Alternatives: Recommendations from Life Cycle Assessments, Report (1 December 2022), https://wedocs.unep.org/handle/20.500.11822/41543
United Nations Environment Programme (2023) Chemicals in Plastics. A Technical Report, Report (3 May 2023), https://wedocs.unep.org/handle/20.500.11822/42366
United Nations Environment Programme (2023) Turning off the Tap. How the world can end plastic pollution and create a circular economy, Report (16 May 2023), https://www.unep.org/resources/turning-off-tap-end-plastic-pollution-create-circular-economy
United Nations Environment Programme (2024) UNEP organization chart (22 August 2024), https://wedocs.unep.org/bitstream/handle/20.500.11822/35352/UNEPOrg.pdf?sequence=4&isAllowed=y
United Nations Environment Programme (2024) Budget overview for the period 2024 – 2025, UNEP/PP/INC.5/INF/2 (22 November 2024)
United Nations Environment Programme (2025) Report of the intergovernmental negotiating committee to develop an international legally binding instrument on plastic pollution, including in the marine environment, on the work of its resumed fifth session, UNEP/PP/INC.5/9 (10 September 2025)
United Nations General Assembly (1972) Institutional and financial arrangements for international environmental cooperation, G.A. Res. A/RES/27/2997 (15 December 1972)
United Nations General Assembly (1992) Report of the United Nations Conference on Environment and Development, Rio de Janeiro, 3–14 June 1992, G.A. Report A/CONF.151/26, Vol. I, Resolutions adopted by the Conference (United Nations publication, Sales No. E.93.I.8 and corrigendum), Resolution 1, Annex I
United Nations General Assembly (2000) United Nations Millennium Declaration, G.A. RES/55/2 (18 September 2000)
United Nations General Assembly (2013) Change of the designation of the Governing Council of the United Nations Environment Programme, G.A. Res. A/RES/67/251 (25 July 2013)
United Nations General Assembly (2015) Transforming our world: the 2030 Agenda for Sustainable Development, G.A. Res. A/RES/70/1 (21 October 2015)
United Nations General Assembly (2022) Report of the United Nations Environment Assembly of the United Nations Environment Programme, resumed fifth session, Nairobi, 28 February to 2 March 2022, A/77/25

Urho N, Ivanova M, Dubrova A, Escobar-Pemberthy N (2019) International environmental governance. Accomplishments and way forward. Nordisk Ministerråd, Copenhagen

Van Berkel R (2011) Evaluation of the global implementation of the UNIDO-UNEP National Cleaner Production Centres (NCPC) Programme. Clean Techn Environ Policy 13:161–175

Van Ewijk S, Stegemann JA (2016) Limitations of the waste hierarchy for achieving absolute reductions in material throughput. J Clean Prod 132:122–128

Vedder C (2018) Art. 5 EUV. In: Vedder C, Heintschel von Heinegg W (eds) Europäisches Unionsrecht, 2nd edn. C.H. Beck, München

Vijge MJ (2010) Towards a world environment organisation. Identifying the barriers to international environmental governance reform. Global Governance Working Paper 40

Vogelsang JN (2023) Warenvernichtung als Rechtsproblem. Unter besonderer Berücksichtigung der kreislaufwirtschaftsrechtlichen Obhutspflicht, Universitätsverlag Göttingen, Göttingen

Völker T, Kovacic Z, Strand R (2020) Indicator development as a site of collective imagination? The case of European Commission policies on the circular economy. Cult Organ 26:103–120

Voorthuis J, Gijbels C (2010) A fair accord: cradle to cradle as a design theory measured against John Rawls' theory of justice and Immanuel Kant's categorical imperative. Sustainability 2:371–382

Wagner L, Langer G (2025a) Die neue Kreislaufwirtschaft, eine Chance für Europa, die Bundesrepublik Deutschland unf die Kommunen. AbfallR 5: 223–230

Wagner L, Langer G (2025b) Die neue Kreislaufwirtschaft, eine Chance für Europa, die Bundesrepublik Deutschland unf die Kommunen (Teil 2). AbfallR 6: 307–314

Weiss F, Scherzer B (2015) (Existance of) common or universal principles of resource management (?). In: Bungenberg M, Hobe S (eds) Permanent sovereignty over natural resources. Springer, Cham, pp 29–60

Wendenburg H (2019) Plastikmüll – ein zentrales Problem des Meeresumweltschutzes. In: Jaeckel L (ed) Ressourcen im globalen Kontext. Schutz und nachhaltige Nutzung. Mohr Siebeck, Tübingen, pp 83–92

Wendenburg H (2023) Normungsroadmap Circular Economy – Rechtsetzung und Standards in der EU und DE. AbfallR 6:254–265

Wibisana AG (2006) Three principles of environmental law: the polluter pays principle, the principle of prevention, and the precautionary principle. In: Faure M, Niessen N (eds) Environmental law in development. Lessons from the Indonesian experience. Edward Elgar Publishing, Cheltenham, pp 24–76

Wong CWY, Lai K, Lun YHV, Cheng TCE (2016) Environmental management. The supply chain perspective. Springer, Cham

Woolcock S (2012) European Union economic diplomacy. The role of the EU in external economic relations. Routledge, Milton Park, Abingdon, Oxon

Zhang X, Liu X, Zhang Y, Xu X, Xiao J, Luh D (2023) Assessing the feasibility of practical cradle to cradle in sustainable conceptual product design. Sustainability 15(6755):1–32

MIX
Papier aus verantwortungsvollen Quellen
Paper from responsible sources
FSC® C105338

If you have any concerns about our products,
you can contact us on
ProductSafety@springernature.com

In case Publisher is established outside the EU,
the EU authorized representative is:
Springer Nature Customer Service Center GmbH
Europaplatz 3, 69115 Heidelberg, Germany

Printed by Libri Plureos GmbH
in Hamburg, Germany